ROCK IT!

STEVE REIFMAN

ROCK IT!

STEVE REIFMAN

TRANSFORM CLASSROOM LEARNING WITH
MOVEMENT, SONGS, AND STORIES

BRIGANTINE MEDIA

Published by Brigantine Media
211 North Avenue, Saint Johnsbury, Vermont 05819

Cover and book design by Jacob L. Grant

Printed in Canada

To order multiple copies of the physical book or the digital download, or for more
information about Brigantine Media educational materials, please contact:

Brigantine Media
211 North Avenue
Saint Johnsbury, Vermont 05819
Phone: 802-751-8802
E-mail: neil@brigantinemedia.com
Website: **www.brigantinemedia.com**

ISBN: 978-1-9384062-0-1

Dedication

To Mom, Dad, Lynn, Jeff, Sylvia, Alan, Ari, and Jordy

Acknowledgments

To my wonderful friends at the Elementary Physical Education Workshop in San Luis Obispo, California. For 18 consecutive summers you have made this conference my favorite week of the year. My passion for using movement, songs, and stories in the classroom was sparked at EPEW, and I am so grateful to everyone who has inspired and encouraged me.

To Janis, Neil, and the entire Brigantine Media team for your terrific work in making this book a reality. It has been a true pleasure working with you.

To Justin Baeder and Rob Plevin for your enthusiastic support of this project and for creating the online workshops that have allowed me to share these ideas with fellow educators.

To my trusted team of "go to" people who freely offer their time, talent, experience, and wisdom whenever I call, e-mail, find them in the hallways at school, or approach them at the gym.

To my battery-charging students who played a valuable role in shaping the ideas in this book.

To the authors and presenters referenced in this book. It has been a joy to discover your work. The Brigantine Media team and I have gone to great lengths to cite everything accurately and determine the proper origin of all the ideas I mention. In the event that we missed something, please let us know, and we will happily make the necessary changes in the digital version of this book.

CONTENTS

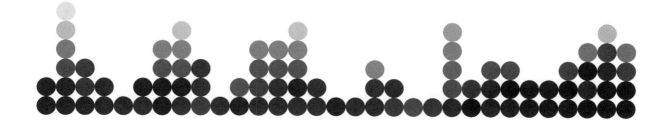

INTRODUCTION

The results of recent brain research have strong implications for improving student learning. Today, we know more than ever about how the brain functions, how students learn best, and which types of instructional practices hold the most promise.

Three types of effective, brain-friendly instructional practices stand out as unusually engaging and powerful for our students—those involving movement, songs, and stories. These strategies have the potential to transform elementary classrooms everywhere.

Children react differently to activities that include movement, songs, and stories. Students become emotionally involved, pay closer attention, and remember more. Educator Jeff Haebig explains that emotions drive attention and attention drives learning. The activities in this book resonate with children on an emotional level, engage them deeply, and enable them to make a personal connection with academic content.

Strategies that incorporate movement, songs, and stories can also improve class morale, build self-esteem and enthusiasm for learning, and increase feelings of student "connectedness" to the class and to one another. This bonding effect is important. Many kids experience the happiness and satisfaction that come from being a valued member of a successful team—playing Little League baseball, performing in a youth orchestra, or acting in a school play. Our classrooms can provide the same kind of bonding experience with the addition of the activities in this book.

And these activities are an absolute blast! The novelty, excitement, and joy they offer turn a potentially dry academic lesson into an engaging, multi-modal experience that kids will remember. These activities create situations where children are completely focused and well-behaved, work with purpose, and learn enthusiastically. I'm not sure how we can beat that. It also doesn't hurt that most of the activities require little to no preparation.

Once teachers begin thinking about how to improve academic instruction through the lens of movement, songs, and stories, we unleash our creativity, and effective ideas develop quickly. Whenever I encounter new concepts that kids are expected to learn, especially those that are abstract or confusing or that would otherwise require rote learning, I ask myself: "Is there a way I can teach this concept using movement? Singing songs? Telling stories?"

Teaching is a difficult, demanding job, and we need to find pleasure in our work to be at our best in the classroom. Movement, songs, and stories can really help our students learn, and what's even better, we can all have fun along the way. Enjoy!

CHAPTER 1

MOVEMENT WARM-UPS

WARM-UPS

- **MORNING WARM-UP**
- **SUBJECT AREA WARM-UPS**

Movement is key to getting students ready to learn. Movement energizes, activates, and helps children focus on the task at hand. For kids who tend to sit passively or become distracted easily, movement is a powerful learning catalyst.

Starting the day with a Morning Warm-Up prepares everyone for a productive day of learning. Subject Area Warm-Ups take place throughout the day when it's time for kids to transition to a new class period or academic topic.

These warm-up routines prepare the students and the teacher mentally and physically for productive work sessions. They can become important class rituals that unite a community of learners and provide a sense of consistency and predictability that many children find reassuring and calming. Some students even perform these routines on their own at other times during the day or after school when they work on their homework.

![icon] MOVEMENT ●●●●●●●●●●●●●●●●●●●●●●●●●●●●●●●●●●●●
MORNING WARM-UP

A consistent, effective morning routine helps set the tone for the school day and prepares children for learning. The morning movement warm-up is part of that morning routine.

Warming up with these movements adds a physical component to the morning routine that both energizes and de-stresses children. Consisting of four parts, this sequence of movements prepares students mentally and physically to have a productive school day by helping them achieve an ideal mind-set for learning—calm, relaxed, focused, and confident.

FROM
STEVE'S CLASSROOM

The first ten minutes of my school day are designed to reach and teach the whole child. Here's my morning routine:

1   A quick morning check-in that addresses the affective domain. It builds a sense of inclusion and mutual caring, strengthens teamwork, increases class bonding, and helps each child feel acknowledged and valued.

2   Three types of class discussions that focus on moral and character development and emphasize strong work habits and social skills. The goals of these brief conversations are to inspire children to maximize their potential, build a sense of purpose, and increase student motivation to learn and succeed.

3   The Morning Warm-Up!

SEQUENCE

There are four parts to the Morning Warm-Up:

1   Cross Crawls

2   Movement Choices

3   Deep Breathing

4   Hook-Ups

1. CROSS CRAWLS

Start the morning movement warm-up with Cross Crawls. It is the most active of the four parts, and it energizes, and even wakes up, students who enter class feeling a bit sleepy. The Cross Crawls movement comes from Paul Dennison's Brain Gym® program.

PROCEDURE:

- Here's how Brain Gym® describes how to perform the Cross Crawls movement: "Stand comfortably and reach across the midline of your body as you alternately move one arm and its opposite leg, then the other arm and leg, rhythmically touching each hand or elbow to the opposite knee." (Dennison and Dennison, 30)

- Do Cross Crawls slowly, with excellent posture and clean contact between the elbow and knee. Have your class perform this movement for 30-45 seconds.

- Many kids tend to speed up while doing Cross Crawls, thinking that faster is better. Emphasize the importance of moving slowly as they alternate connecting their elbows to their opposite knees.

In her book *Smart Moves: Why Learning Is Not All in Your Head,* neurophysiologist and author Dr. Carla Hannaford says that when children perform Cross Crawls regularly, "more nerve networks form and myelinate in the corpus callosum, thus making communication between the two hemispheres faster and more integrated for high level reasoning." Moving slowly, Hannaford says, "requires fine motor involvement and balance, consciously activating the vestibular system and frontal lobes."

2. MOVEMENT CHOICES

Give students a choice of five movements, as recommended by self-described "Body/ Brain Boogie Man" Jeff Haebig. This section of the warm-up is a transitional step, in which children choose the type of movement they want to do, based on what they need at this time. If they need further energizing, they should opt for A. If they already feel energized and ready to go, they should choose B or E. Choices C and D are available for kids whose needs fall somewhere in between.

The five movement choices include:

A ENERGIZERS
From a standing position, keep the upper body straight and move the head toward the left side of the waist at a 45 degree angle, come back up, then down to the right side of the waist, come back up, and repeat. Energizers are big, bouncy, angular movements.

B CALMERS
From a standing position, bend at the waist and slowly rock the body forward and back. Haebig uses the phrase, "Rock it to calm it," to describe this movement.

> *FROM*
> ## STEVE'S CLASSROOM
>
> Haebig points out that when students tip back in their chairs, many of them are trying to achieve a calming effect. Armed with this insight, I now invite students who rock in their chairs to stand and rock to avoid the chance of falling backwards. They are even welcome to step outside the classroom if they want to stand and rock privately.

C ENERGIZE AND CALM COMBO
Combine the first two in order to achieve both an energizing and calming effect.

D STOP 'N' GO
Select any of the previous choices and pause periodically.

E NO, THANK YOU, I PREFER TO WATCH
Some students do not need to move and should not be pressured into doing so. Standing still while others move is a perfectly legitimate choice that teachers need to honor.

3. DEEP BREATHING

Now that students have had the opportunity to energize their bodies during the first two parts of the warm-up, the goal is to help them become calm and relaxed.

PROCEDURE:

- Stand tall with one hand on the belly button and the other hand on the upper chest. Students close their eyes to help focus on themselves.

- There are three variations of deep breathing to try, all adapted from Jeff Haebig:

    - Nose vs. Mouth Breathing: Breathe in and out through only the nose, then through only the mouth, then breathe in through the nose and out through the mouth, and breathe in through the mouth and out through the nose. Explore these variations either in one session or over a period of days.

    - Alternate Nose Breathing: Inhale and exhale while holding one nostril closed and then switching nostrils.

    - Rhythmic Breathing: Inhale and exhale for a certain number of counts. It requires a strong internal focus and helps students develop breath control. Start with a few counts and increase the number as students gain proficiency.

FROM
STEVE'S CLASSROOM

Many kids are curious about what's going on around them and are easily distracted, so closing the eyes is necessary to help them focus their attention internally, not externally.

MORNING WARM-UP

4. HOOK-UPS

Hook-ups are also from the Brain Gym® program by Dennison and Dennison.

PROCEDURE:

- "Part I: Cross your ankles. Next, extend your arms in front of you and cross one wrist over the other; then interlace your fingers and draw your clasped hands up toward your chest. Hold like this for a minute or more, breathing slowly, with your eyes open or closed. As you inhale, touch the tip of your tongue to the roof of your mouth at the hard palate (just behind the teeth), and relax your tongue on exhalation.

- "Part II: When ready, uncross your arms and legs and put your fingertips together in front of your chest, continuing to breathe deeply for another minute and hold the tip of your tongue on the roof of your mouth when you inhale." (Dennison and Dennison, 68)

FROM
STEVE'S CLASSROOM

I recall one young boy who frequently got in trouble with previous teachers because focusing for an extended period of time was extremely difficult for him. He would become fidgety and distracting and his stress level would rise, which made it even harder for him to focus. One day I told him that he could go outside anytime he felt he was losing focus and do one of the morning movements. He learned to get up from his chair on his own, step outside, and come back in a minute ready to go. Once he realized that he could do this without my permission and that he was the one in total control of his behavior, his focus and confidence increased significantly.

VARIATIONS:

You can add an extra dimension to this move by having students think about the upcoming day and focus on a specific aspect while standing in this position.

- To build achievement orientation in your students, go through the day's schedule and ask what they hope to accomplish while at school.

- To brighten everyone's mood, ask them to think about the part of the day they are looking forward to the most (it can even be something like playing at recess).

- To improve classroom conduct, have the kids set a behavioral goal that will make a big difference in their day, such as being a better listener or remembering to ask for help when they need it.

- Circulate throughout the room while the kids are in this position and give private, individual encouragement and behavioral reminders.

Now students are fully prepared to sit down and pay attention to the first academic lesson of the day.

MOVEMENT •••••••••••••••••••••••••••••••
SUBJECT AREA WARM-UPS

Warm-ups can be used throughout the day to reinvigorate students as you transition from one subject area to another and prepare them for the specific academic demands and types of thinking that lie ahead.

One routine is designed for the task of writing. It warms up the hands and prepares the mind for this type of work. The other routine is a general-purpose warm-up that can be used before instructional lessons in any subject area.

WRITING WARM-UP

This writing warm-up is adapted from reading specialist Debra Em Wilson and occupational therapist Margot Heiniger-White, co-authors of *S'cool Moves for Learning*. The hand and arm exercises take 30 to 60 seconds to complete. As you lead the class in these movements, encourage the students to think about what they hope to accomplish that day. All seven parts of this routine are performed seated.

1 DOTS

Use the thumb of one hand to push into the palm of the other hand. Each push is considered a "dot." Encourage the students to push dots into every part of the palm. Switch sides and do the same with the other hand.

2 SQUEEZES

Grab the wrist with the opposite hand and gently squeeze. Continue squeezing all the way up to the shoulder and back down to the wrist. Switch sides and repeat on the other arm.

3 RUBBING HANDS

Rub the palms together for a few seconds to generate some heat. Then rub the backs of the hands together in the same way. Spread apart the fingers and slide the fingers of each hand into the openings of the other hand. Turn the hands the other way and slide the fingers of each hand together into the openings of the other hand.

4 CLAPS AND PATS

Clap the hands together and then keep clapping as you slide the hands to the opposite wrists and up the opposite arm. Pat the skin from the wrists all the way up to the shoulders and back down.

5 GLOVES

As if putting on imaginary writing gloves, use the thumb and index finger of one hand to touch the skin of each finger on the opposite hand from fingertip to the wrist. Switch sides and repeat with the other hand.

6 GRAB AND RESIST

Interlace the fingers of each hand and push the palms together. Pull the hands away from each other, but don't let go. Resisting in this manner will work the shoulders and upper back.

7 TRANSITION TO LISTENING POSITION

With the hands still attached from the previous movement, have students put their hands under their chins and elbows on their knees and look up at the teacher. This greatly increases the eye contact between the students and the teacher as the instructional lesson begins.

GENERAL ACTIVITY WARM-UP

This warm-up sequence is adapted from physical education instructor Chip Candy and can be used to kick off any lesson. Have students perform this routine twice while seated on the floor.

PROCEDURE:

- Students alternate hands and touch their opposite ears, shoulders, hips, knees, and feet. In doing so, every move they make crosses the midline as they go from their heads to their feet. Specifically, the kids touch their right hands to their left ears, left hands to their right ears, right hands to left shoulders, left hand to right shoulders, right hands to left hips, left hands to right hips, right hands to left knees, left hands to right knees, right hands to left feet, and left hands to right feet. They say the name of each body part as they touch it.

- After the final move, the students say, "PACE," which is an acronym to promote attentive listening.

  P osture

  A ttention

  C areful listening

  E ye contact

- As the kids say "PACE," they put their hands under their chins and elbows on their knees and look up at the board.

- If your students proceed through this sequence twice, the warm-up routine sounds like this: "Ear, ear, shoulder, shoulder, hip, hip, knee, knee, foot, foot, ear, ear, shoulder, shoulder, hip, hip, knee, knee, foot, foot, PACE!"

And now everyone's ready to get to work.

FROM
STEVE'S CLASSROOM

One day, a student suggested that our class have a social studies warm-up. This young go-getter then went home and created a sequence that she was excited to share with her teammates. (She also launched a class newspaper and will probably create a *Fortune* 500 company one day.) I encourage you to invite students to offer their own ideas, recognize these efforts publicly when they happen, and honor children who care so much and invest themselves so deeply in their learning.

CHAPTER 2

TEACHING MATH
WITH MOVEMENT AND STORIES

MOVEMENT

Using movement to create high-quality learning experiences is like making banana pancakes. The first time I ate banana pancakes they were delicious. The fruit was mixed into the batter, and I could taste both banana and pancake in every bite. The next time I had banana pancakes, the bananas were on top of the stack, not scattered throughout the pancakes. My breakfast tasted different. Still good, but not great.

When you add movement to what would otherwise be a sedentary activity, it's like laying the bananas on top of the pancakes. It's good, but not great. Imagine that your students are sitting at their desks working on math problems. It will take them 20 minutes to work through the assignment. Halfway through, ask your students to move to a location on the other side of the room and then continue working. This physical move helps them learn for several reasons: the novelty of switching seats increases student alertness, the transition time to a new spot gives everyone a needed break, and the new frame of reference provided by the second location—what authors Traci Lengel and Mike Kuczala, in their book *The Kinesthetic Classroom*, call an "environmental address"—offers students a different context.

But you can improve learning even more when specific types of movement are embedded into learning activities. That's like mixing the bananas directly into the pancake batter. When the activity features a type of movement that represents, matches, or embodies the meaning of the content, students will learn even more. The result: far more flavor and far more impact. Serve the tasty banana pancakes whenever you can!

MOVEMENT ●●●●●●●●●●●●●●●●●●●●●●●●●●●●●●●
PLACE VALUE HOPSCOTCH

Many children have difficulty understanding the place value system. Typically, either kids don't know the names of the various place value positions, or they don't understand the meaning of each place. This activity helps students learn the names of the place value positions and can easily be adapted to incorporate as many places as you are teaching. (When your students are ready to learn the places to the right of the decimal point, try the next activity, the Place Value Shuffle, page 20.)

COMMON CORE STANDARDS

CCSS.Math.Content.1.NBT.B.2
CCSS.Math.Content.2.NBT.A.1
CCSS.Math.Content.3.NBT.A.2
CCSS.Math.Content.4.NBT.A.1
CCSS.Math.Content.5.NBT.A.1

PREPARATION:

- Make outdoor Place Value Hopscotch courts with sidewalk chalk or paint (use paint only if you have tenure, a solid reputation, and a strong relationship with your principal!).

- The more courts you make, the more turns students will get, the less time they will spend waiting, and the easier the activity will be to manage.

- To make courts inside, use painter's tape to create courts on the floor.

- You can make "virtual courts" by drawing the design of the Place Value Hopscotch court on the board. Have a few students at a time call out the names of the positions as they make a series of short hops on the floor, following the drawing on the board. Virtual courts require just a few feet of open space to play and the least amount of preparation time.

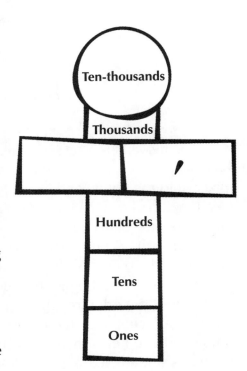

PROCEDURE:

- As students jump into each box, they call out the name written in that box. With the first three boxes, the kids call out "ones," "tens," and "hundreds." The next box is the double jump for the comma, and the children say the word "comma" aloud as they land on this spot. The last two boxes are "thousands" and "ten thousands."

Jumping through the hopscotch courts gives kids an opportunity to use multiple learning modalities as they see, say, hear, and move through the names of the place value positions simultaneously. To maximize learning, students should repeat this sequence several times over a period of days.

MOVEMENT ●●●●●●●●●●●●●●●●●●●●●●●●●●●●●●●●
PLACE VALUE SHUFFLE

The Place Value Shuffle helps students learn the tenths and hundredths places to the right of the decimal point. When students are learning these, it is easier for them to understand the meanings and relative sizes of the place value positions by moving side-to-side, as opposed to moving forward as in Place Value Hopscotch. The horizontal arrangement of boxes provides a more accurate picture.

COMMON CORE STANDARDS

CCSS.Math.Content.4.NF.C.6
CCSS.Math.Content.5.NBT.A.1
CCSS.Math.Content.5.NBT.A.3

| Hundreds | Tens | Ones | | Tenths | Hundredths |

PREPARATION:

- Create the court as shown, using chalk, painter's tape, or as "virtual courts" on the board.

PROCEDURE:

- Have the children begin by standing on the hundreds spot. They shuffle, or sidestep, to the right and say the name of each place until they arrive at the final spot, the hundredths.

- Everyone yells the word "and" when they step on the decimal point, to reinforce the idea that the only appropriate use of the word "and" when saying a large number is in reference to the decimal point.

- The kids can exit the court after stepping on the hundredths place, or you can have them slide back to the left and say the positions in the opposite order.

The Place Value Shuffle resembles a popular exercise that athletes do to improve their lateral movement. Many students enjoy the activity even more when they know that. As the kids gain proficiency with the shuffle, encourage them to pick up the pace—a speed component will add some sizzle!

VARIATIONS:

There are other steps you can take (pun intended) to aid in children's conceptual understanding of place value.

- Rather than write the place value position names in boxes of roughly equal size, create boxes that decrease in size as you proceed from left to right.

- Along with the name of the place value positions, you can draw common pictorial representations of each position (e.g., cubes to show ones, sticks to show tens, flats to show hundreds, and blocks to show thousands) in the spaces to help students connect the meaning of each term to its size.

- You can add another movement component to this activity by having students adjust the height of their bodies as they move through each place value position to match their physical size with the meaning of each place. Students stand up tall and spread their arms and legs out wide in the hundreds place and gradually become shorter and bring their arms and legs in as they move to the right, until they are practically kneeling as they enter the hundredths place.

- If you want your students to move exclusively in a horizontal direction, you can combine Place Value Hopscotch and the Place Value Shuffle to make one long horizontal court that starts on the left with the ten-thousands and moves to the right through the decimal point to the hundredths.

MOVEMENT •••••••••••••••••••••••••••••••
PLACE VALUE JUMPING JACKS

This activity reinforces the meaning of each place value position as well as the place value system as a whole.

COMMON CORE STANDARDS

CCSS.Math.Content.1.NBT.B.2
CCSS.Math.Content.2.NBT.A.1
CCSS.Math.Content.5.NBT.A.1

PREPARATION:

You will need open space for this exercise, especially to the left of each child.

PROCEDURE:

- Students begin in the ones place and count from 1 to 10 as they do ten jumping jacks.

- At "10," the kids wrap their arms around their bodies in a tight bear hug, simulating how ten ones come together to form one ten.

- In unison, the kids hop to the left, showing how the stick of ten must be moved from the ones place into the tens place. The kids then do ten more jumping jacks, this time continuing their counting where they left off and counting by tens from 10 to 100.

- At 100, the kids again hug themselves, showing how 10 tens become one hundred. This time the hug is a little wider because they are now representing 100 objects. The kids then hop to the left, showing how the hundred must be moved into the hundreds place.

- The pattern is repeated for as many positions as you wish. Instead of full jumping jacks, tired kids (and teachers) may do "half-jacks" by bringing their arms only to shoulder height. Extremely tired people may opt for "finger jacks."

A chart on the board (see page 23) showing the multiples in each place helps everyone follow along with the activity and learn the place value concept (that each place is ten times greater than the one to its right) as they physically move through each position.

PLACE VALUE JUMPING JACKS

Ten Thousands	Thousands	Hundreds	Tens	Ones
10,000	1,000	100	10	1
20,000	2,000	200	20	2
30,000	3,000	300	30	3
40,000	4,000	400	40	4
50,000	5,000	500	50	5
60,000	6,000	600	60	6
70,000	7,000	700	70	7
80,000	8,000	800	80	8
90,000	9,000	900	90	9

MOVEMENT ●●●●●●●●●●●●●●●●●●●●●●●●●●●●●●●
JUMP ROPES FOR MATH

Manuvering jump ropes into shapes helps kids understand a number of curricular concepts. When using jump ropes, yarn, or string to make geometric shapes and numbers, kids often pay more attention to detail and respond to your challenges with greater care and craftsmanship than they do when using paper and pencil.

PROCEDURE:

- Students lay out jump ropes (or long pieces of yarn or string) to form different numbers or geometric shapes.

- Use this strategy any time you believe students would benefit from a break from paper-and-pencil activities in favor of a more kinesthetic approach.

COMMON CORE STANDARDS
CCSS.Math.Content.K.CC.A.3
CCSS.Math.Content.K.G.A.2
CCSS.Math.Content.K.G.B.5
CCSS.Math.Content.K.G.B.6
CCSS.Math.Content.1.G.A.2
CCSS.Math.Content.2.G.A.1
CCSS.Math.Content.3.G.A.1
CCSS.Math.Content.4.G.A.1

Issuing challenges in an inquiry-based manner is the most effective way to use the jump ropes.

- When studying geometric shapes, ask, "Can you arrange your jump rope in the shape of a pentagon? Hexagon? Octagon?"

- When studying angles, ask, "With your jump rope, can you form a right angle? An acute angle? An obtuse angle?"

This strategy also works for letters and words (see page 54).

MOVEMENT ●●●●●●●●●●●●●●●●●●●●●●●●●●● RAPID ROUNDING

The concept of rounding can sometimes be confusing. Moving on a life-sized number line helps students understand how it works.

PREPARATION:

- Create a number line on the playground with sidewalk chalk or on the classroom floor with painter's tape, or draw a number line on the board and have the kids spread themselves out in the classroom on their own "virtual number lines."

- Each number line should have eleven spaces so that, for example, a line would go from 30 to 40 or 70 to 80.

> **COMMON CORE STANDARDS**
>
> CCSS.Math.Content.3.NBT.A.1
> CCSS.Math.Content.4.NBT.A.3
> CCSS.Math.Content.5.NBT.A.4

PROCEDURE:

- Once you have chosen the range of values for each number line, begin every round of the game by having students stand on a predetermined spot on the number line.

- Example: if the number line goes from 30 to 40, have the students start on the number 39. On the "go" signal, the children round to the nearest ten by moving up to the number 40. If you start on 32, they move down to 30.

- You may choose to have the students move all at once or in smaller, easier-to-manage shifts. By watching this activity, you will know which children need individual follow-up with the rounding concept.

Many students make the mistake of rounding a number like 36 down to 30 instead of up to 40. Physically moving forward or backward on a number line clears up this problem because students think about the concept of rounding in terms of actual distance. Beginning at 36 on the physical number line, students need to move only four spots to get to 40, but six spots to get to 30. You can also use this activity to explain the convention for rounding up. Have students stand in the middle of the number line, for example, at 35 on a number line from 30 to 40. The physical distance, of course, is the same from 30 to 35 as it is from 35 to 40, and many kids will be confused. Explain that mathematicians solved this problem many years ago by agreeing to round up in these cases.

MOVEMENT ●●●●●●●●●●●●●●●●●●●●●●●●●●●●●●
THE HUNGRY ALLIGATOR

When teaching students the "greater than" and "less than" signs, show them that the signs are like the mouth of a hungry alligator—and the alligator always wants to eat the larger number. This game works for all kinds of numbers.

COMMON CORE STANDARDS

CCSS.Math.Content.1.NBT.B.3
CCSS.Math.Content.2.NBT.A.4
CCSS.Math.Content.3.NF.A.3d
CCSS.Math.Content.4.NF.A.2
CCSS.Math.Content.4.NF.C.7
CCSS.Math.Content.5.NBT.A.3

PREPARATION:

- Have each student print any number neatly on an index card or small dry-erase board. Use the type of numbers for your needs—one-, two- or three-digit numbers or larger, or even fractions or decimals.

PROCEDURE:

- The students form two lines with about five feet of space between them. They turn and face each other so that each student is directly across from a partner and then hold up their numbers in front of them.

- Choose a student volunteer to be the first "hungry alligator." The first alligator takes a turn proceeding through the two lines.

- At each pair of students, the alligator looks at the two cards and must determine the larger one.

- The student then turns, faces the larger number, and makes a sideways "V" by holding out his or her arms.

- Once the first alligator finishes the course, that student switches spots with someone in line and that child becomes the new alligator. Have the kids on one side of the line move one place to their left so that the same comparisons aren't repeated. This activity moves fairly quickly and offers teachers a great opportunity to check student understanding.

In a large classroom, it may be best to create two or three courses in order to provide every child with a turn as the hungry alligator. You may want to spread this activity out over a few days, doing it for a few minutes each session, so that everyone gets a turn and the class has multiple opportunities to reinforce this skill.

348   152

MOVEMENT ●●●●●●●●●●●●●●●●●●●●●●●●●●●●●●●●
READING LARGE NUMBERS

Reading large numbers is a difficult task for many children to learn. With this strategy, students incorporate a series of hand movements into the reading process to simplify the challenge into a number of smaller, more manageable steps.

> **COMMON CORE STANDARDS**
>
> **CCSS.Math.Content.2.NBT.A.3**

PROCEDURE:

Example: 53,876

- Students say "fifty-three," clap on the word "thousand," say "eight," snap on the word "hundred," and say "seventy-six."

- Prompt the students by writing the number on the board and pointing to the comma when the students say "thousand" and clap.

- Students can add another hand motion: flatten their hands with thumbs touching their chests as they say two-part numbers such as "fifty-three" and "seventy-six." This mimics the hyphen that is needed for all two-part numbers between twenty-one and ninety-nine written in word form (as opposed to one-part numbers such as "thirty").

- To build the habit of reading larger numbers in this manner, repeat this process three times for each large number you encounter.

VARIATION:

- You can use this same approach when working with decimals.

Example: 1.74

- Students say, "one and seventy-four hundredths."

- On the word "and," students make a decimal point with the tip of their fingers. They make the hyphen with a flat hand when saying "seventy-four." When saying "hundredths," the children make the shape of a little square with four fingers of one hand. Because it takes 100 of these squares to fill one 10 x 10 grid, this finger movement helps students develop conceptual understanding of hundredths.

- In addition, students can form tenths by extending their index fingers, since 10 little squares would connect to form a bar approximately that size.

STORIES

M ovie producer Peter Guber, in a March 15, 2011 *Psychology Today* article entitled "The Inside Story," writes that stories offer ". . . far more than entertainment. They are the most effective form of human communication, more powerful than any other way of packaging information. And telling purposeful stories is certainly the most efficient means of persuasion in everyday life, the most effective way of translating ideas into action, whether you're green-lighting a $90 million film project, motivating employees to meet an important deadline, or getting your kids through a crisis."

STORIES ●●●●●●●●●●●●●●●●●●●●●●●●●●●●●
THE SUBTRACTION FIRE

If you teach re-grouping as a subtraction strategy, "The Subtraction Fire" story helps students learn why subtraction with regrouping works. Without a strong conceptual understanding of subtraction, many kids have the tendency to subtract the top digit from the bottom in the ones, tens, and hundreds place rather than the bottom from the top.

COMMON CORE STANDARDS

CCSS.Math.Content.2.NBT.B.5
CCSS.Math.Content.2.NBT.B.7
CCSS.Math.Content.3.NBT.A.2
CCSS.Math.Content.4.NBT.B.4

STORY

There are big castle walls separating each place value position or "column" from the others and within each set of walls lies an individual Place Value kingdom. The smallest kingdom is on the right, and it is home to little creatures called Ones. Living next to the ones are the slightly larger Tens. The larger Hundreds live one place over to the left. Finally, the humongous Thousands occupy the far left kingdom.

A fire burns brightly at the top of each wall as a symbol of the intelligence of all the Place Value children that live below in their respective kingdoms. Like the creatures themselves, the fires start small but increase in size and strength as one proceeds from right to left.

Normally, the citizens of each kingdom stay within their own walls, but in times of trouble—such as when they need to subtract—they are there to help one another.

$$
\begin{array}{c|c|c|c}
4 & 2 & 3 & 7 \\
-\,2 & 5 & 6 & 9 \\
\hline
\end{array}
$$

PROCEDURE:

- Now the stage is set for some actual subtraction. Use your best acting skills for this one and ham it up! For example:

$$\begin{array}{r} 4{,}237 \\ -\,2{,}569 \\ \hline \end{array}$$

- Start in the Ones place. Ask, "Can we subtract nine from seven?"

- When it's clear you can't, pretend to be a citizen of the Ones kingdom and turn to your left to face the Tens. Cup your hands around your mouth, take a deep inhale, and pretend to scream to your neighbors, "Hey, Tens, may we borrow one of you to help us subtract?"

- Then move into the Tens kingdom, turn back to face the Ones, and give yourself an answer by cupping your hands around your mouth and yelling, "Sure!"

- Return home to the Ones and breathe a sigh of relief because your subtraction need has just been met by your kind neighbors.

- Draw visual representations on the board of each digit in the top number to help children make sense of the borrowing process.

- Reach over to the Tens place and borrow a stick of ten. Then move the stick of ten over the kingdom wall separating the tens place from the ones. As the stick of ten flies over the kingdom wall, the fire melts the glue binding the little squares in the stick and turns it into ten individual ones. Add those ten ones to the seven already there, and subtract nine from seventeen.

- Repeat this process two more times, and each time the increasingly larger fire is there to melt the glue holding the increasingly larger pieces together so that the pieces fit with their new friends and allow subtraction to occur.

Seeing the fire "melt" the glue reminds students that borrowing is a necessary step when subtracting a larger number from a smaller one. The smaller number needs help, and the only place to get that help is in the place or places to the left. In the days after you first present the Subtraction Fire, you may find students drawing little fires and walls on their papers to assist them with subtraction.

FROM
STEVE'S CLASSROOM

As children, most of us were probably taught to use standard algorithms to solve computation problems. The drawback of this traditional approach is that many kids carry out memorized procedures without understanding the rationale behind them. Cognitively Guided Instruction (CGI) is one of many programs that promote an alternative approach that emphasizes the importance of developing strong number sense and encourages students to choose strategies that make sense to them, not simply ones they have memorized. If students do choose to use a standard algorithm, however, they need to perform the steps correctly. "The Subtraction Fire" is one of several ideas in this book that help children do just that.

STORIES ●●●●●●●●●●●●●●●●●●●●●●●●●●●●●●●●●●●●●
AND THEN ALONG CAME...

This story reinforces place value concepts. Students work alone or in pairs. They need place value mats and number tiles.

> **COMMON CORE STANDARDS**
>
> **CCSS.Math.Content.1.NBT.B.2**
> **CCSS.Math.Content.2.NBT.A.1**

STORY

Jessie is walking through her neighborhood, trying to raise money for her favorite charity.	Select a student to be the main character in the story (Jessie).
And then along came . . . Trevor, who offers to donate $8.	Choose a student (Trevor). The students smile and nod approvingly at Trevor, and then put the "8" tile in the ones place. Quickly check everyone's board before continuing with the story and provide any necessary feedback.
And then along came . . . Chris, who gives her $20.	Choose another student (Chris). Chris grins and is feeling pretty good about himself. Your students put a 2 in the tens place.
And then along came . . . J.P., who tells Jessie that he wants to buy a new toy and has the nerve to ask to borrow $9.	Choose another student (J.P.) Your students shake their heads at J.P. and adjust their boards to show $19, while you also shake your head at J.P. and once again scan the room to check for accuracy.

Because kids become so interested in Jessie's endeavor and listening for their own names to be used, you can keep this going for quite a while. Sometimes you add to Jessie's total, other times you subtract, but every time, keep it entertaining and come up with storylines that capture the personalities of the students in your class and maybe even give a boost to those who may need one. Along the way the kids are gaining authentic math experience working with place value positions.

Here's an easy way to ensure you are randomly selecting students: Print each child's name on a Popsicle stick, then fill a cup with the sticks. Draw a stick when you need to choose a student at random. Every time you draw a stick, remove it from the cup until all sticks have been chosen. Then refill the cup. This strategy ensures that everyone receives an equal opportunity to participate.

STORIES ●●●●●●●●●●●●●●●●●●●●●●●●●●●●●●●●
THE DAY STEVEN GOT EVEN

This story works well to begin instruction about odd and even numbers, using what developmental psychologist Howard Gardner calls a "narrative entry point" in his book *Multiple Intelligences: The Theory in Practice*.

COMMON CORE STANDARDS

CCSS.Math.Content.2.OA.C.3

STORY

One day at recess Steven went to the doubles handball court and asked to play. His four friends told him they were sorry, but he couldn't play because he didn't have a partner. In a doubles court, they reminded him, teams of two face other teams of two. Steven tried again the next day, this time encountering three established pairs when he arrived at the court and asked to play. Once again, the other kids told him they'd be happy to have him play, but he'd need to find another person because now altogether there were seven people. Seven is an odd number, and Steven would need to find an eighth player in order to make it even.

Undeterred, Steven tried again the next day. This time, before heading to the court, Steven noticed a new student walking alone on the playground and invited the boy to be his partner. When the others saw a beaming Steven show up with another player, they gladly invited the pair to play in the next game. And that happy story, kids, is the day that Steven (literally) got even.

While telling the story, use tally marks to record the number of players present at the court each time Steven arrives. This way, students can easily understand the difference between an even number of tallies, where everyone has a partner, and an odd number of tallies, where Steven is missing a partner. To highlight the contrast, record the odd numbers on the left side of the board and the even numbers on the right.

Kids love this story because they hear the title and initially think it will be one of revenge. Upon finding out that the story has nothing to do with revenge and instead ends happily with Steven being able to play handball with his friends after making an effort to include a new student in the game, the kids have a warm, fuzzy feeling on the inside—and learn the difference between odd and even numbers.

STORIES ●●●●●●●●●●●●●●●●●●●●●●●●●●●●●●●●●●
THE SPRINKLER SYSTEM

This story was by inspired by Cincinnati Bengals wide receiver Chad Ochocinco, who scored a touchdown during a game and celebrated by doing the sprinkler dance. With one hand touching the back of his head and the other extended straight out in front of him, Chad pivoted in different directions pretending to spray the field with water.

I think he must have said to himself, "This would be a great way to teach schoolchildren how to multiply large numbers." I picked up on his message and have used his Sprinkler System ever since to teach the traditional multiplication algorithm.

PREPARATION:

Write a multiplication problem on the board, such as:

$$\begin{array}{r} 4\,2\,7 \\ \times\ \ \ 5 \\ \hline \end{array}$$

Draw a little sprinkler head coming out of the "ground" right next to the 5. Even better, bring in an impact sprinkler if you have one.

STORY

- Explain that the sprinkler generally shoots water straight up in the air before it pivots, so you start by multiplying 5 by 7 because the 5 is spraying the 7 with water. (During this demonstration you are also carrying numbers and recording them as necessary.)

- Then the sprinkler pivots to the left and sprays water at the 2. So the second step is to multiply 5 by 2.

- Finally, the sprinkler pivots again to the left and shoots water at the 4. Now multiply 5 by 4.

- For larger numbers, continue pivoting the sprinkler to the left, one digit at a time, and multiply the bottom number by the additional digits.

Now it's time for you and your students to get up and do Chad's sprinkler dance! Shoot the water straight up and then pivot and shoot as many times as necessary to go along with your number example. Movement *and* a story—now that's a winning combination!

⦿ STORIES ●●●●●●●●●●●●●●●●●●●●●●●●●●●●●●●●
THE MULTIPLICATION HULA

This story helps students learn where to place the decimal point when multiplying decimals or money amounts.

PREPARATION:

Write a multiplication problem like this one on the board:

$$
\begin{array}{r}
6.18 \\
\times \quad 3 \\
\hline
\end{array}
$$

COMMON CORE STANDARDS
CCSS.Math.Content.5.NBT.B.7

STORY

- Do the multiplication problem aloud with your students.

- Instruct your students to start at the decimal point and "hula" to the right for each digit to the right of the decimal point. As you say this, make little loops on the board under the numbers. In this case, since there are two digits to the right of the decimal point, the kids should hula two times.

- Then, physically drop your bodies straight down to show that you are now moving to the product, below the equal sign.

- Finally, starting on the far right side of the product, the kids hula back to the left the same number of times they hula'd to the right and then place the decimal point. Explain that the hula is a balanced dance and that however many times you hula to the right on top, that's how many times you need to hula back to the left on the bottom.

$$
\begin{array}{r}
6.18 \\
\times \quad 3 \\
\hline
18.54
\end{array}
$$

Reinforce the Multiplication Hula with a little theatrics. Wear a Hawaiian shirt and play Hawaiian music in the background when you first describe the Multiplication Hula. After you explain the process of moving the decimal, ask the kids to practice the dance a few times. Make it an event—a special moment that kids will tell their friends and family about: "Look at what we were lucky enough to do today in class!"

We hope that students will use number sense to place the decimal point correctly when multiplying with decimals. They should be able to reason that the product couldn't be $1.854 or $185.4 because those answers wouldn't make sense. Number sense would tell you that the answer to the problem in the example has to be $18.54 because if you have 6 dollars 3 times, the product has to be about $18. The Multiplication Hula is a short-cut, and we must guard against the danger of kids using a shortcut without having conceptual understanding. But this tip can help many children generate or check their answers, especially as they progress through school and begin to encounter more complex multiplication-with-decimals questions (e.g., 23.45 x 1.768). It's a nice trick to have in the bag.

STORIES ●●●●●●●●●●●●●●●●●●●●●●●●●●●●●●●●●●●
THE STORY OF PERI METER

This story introduces the geometric concept of perimeter and combines it with specific physical movements.

COMMON CORE STANDARDS

CCSS.Math.Content.3.MD.D.8

STORY

Once there was a boy named Peri. He was a bit unusual because the only thing he liked to do was walk around the outside edge of every place he visited. At recess, he walked along the border of the playground. At home, he walked around the outside edge of his room.

His mom noticed her son's habit and shared her concern with Mr. Meter, Peri's father. She said, "Honey, I'm worried about Peri. All he wants to do is walk around the edge of things." He told her not to worry about it, but Peri's behavior continued. Finally, they decided that Peri needed to be checked out by a doctor.

After school the next day, the three went to the doctor. As the family waited for the doctor, Mr. Meter read a magazine, Mrs. Meter worried about her son, and Peri just walked around the edge of the waiting room. In the examination room, once Peri stopped walking around it, the doctor determined that Peri was just fine and that the parents should simply leave him alone and take him to have a nice meal. The Meters went to Peri's favorite restaurant, where Peri proceeded to walk a series of laps around the salad bar.

The next day at school, Peri began walking laps around the track. His walking turned into running, and the coach noticed Peri's talent. Over time, Peri became a successful runner and lived happily ever after.

PROCEDURE:

- After you tell the story, ask for a volunteer who'd like to play Peri Meter. Ask that student to go outside and re-enter as Peri Meter.

- When "Peri" comes in, point to a table and say, "Hello, Peri, check out our new table." Peri will (hopefully) start to walk around the table.

- As time allows, choose other volunteers to play the part of Peri Meter so more students can experience the joy of walking around a table. Everyone will laugh, and the image of seeing Peri Meter walk around the table makes the eventual transition to paper-and-pencil perimeter challenges easier.

STORIES ●●●●●●●●●●●●●●●●●●●●●●●●●●●●●●●●
THE STORY OF AREA
(PRONOUNCED "AH • RE • UH")

This story helps bring to life the geometric concept of area and adds specific movements to reinforce the ideas.

> **COMMON CORE STANDARDS**
>
> **CCSS.Math.Content.3.MD.C.5**

STORY

Down the street from Peri lives another interesting individual, a young lady named Area. She doesn't walk around places as Peri does; she likes to lie down on flat things and cover them completely. Luckily for her, she has the ability to change the shape of her body so she can cover even the most unusual objects.

At home, when her mother showed Area the family's new rug, she got on the floor and lay down on it. At school, when her friends played Place Value Hopscotch at recess, Area didn't do any hopping. She lay down on the court. In class, when the teacher passed out place value mats so the kids could learn all the place value positions, you guessed it—Area lay on them.

One day, Area's family went shopping for a new bed for Area's little sister. To Area, the mattress store was like Disneyland. Her eyes lit up at the sight of all the brand-new mattresses. Area started to lie down on every one of them. The store manager noticed Area, and went over to her mother.

"Ma'am, is this your daughter?" he asked.

"Yes, she is," Area's mom replied, thinking he was upset and would ask them to leave the store. She was surprised to see that he couldn't stop smiling.

"Ma'am," he said to her, "your daughter has real talent. I have never seen anyone who lies down as well as she does. Why, she's a natural! I would like to hire her to inspect all the new mattresses as they arrive at the store to ensure that they are fit to sell to customers."

Area's mom was delighted, and the manager hired Area as the store's new mattress inspector. She became a great success and lived happily ever after.

PROCEDURE:

- Ask for a volunteer who'd like to pretend to be Area. Ask the student to go outside and re-enter as Area.

- When the volunteer comes in, point to a nearby table and say, "Hello, Area, check out our new table." Area will undoubtedly climb up on the table in true Area style and spread her arms and legs out to cover it. Everyone will make a big deal about what a good job

Area is doing, and probably for the only time in that student's academic career, he/she will be praised for lying down on the job!

- After a few more students take a turn being Area, you are ready for a magical moment— bringing the concepts of perimeter and area together. Ask one student to be Peri and another to be Area at the same time.

- With one student lying on the desk and the other walking around it at the same time, a powerful image is formed in the students' minds, helping them forever distinguish these two concepts that are often confused. You can pair up the students and give everyone the experience of being both Peri and Area at their desks.

This story and movement experience about Peri and Area helps make a smooth transition to paper-and-pencil work. When determining the area of a shape, some children like to count the individual squares while others multiply the length of the array times the width. Show students the visual of Peri and Area, with Peri marching around the outside of all the beds to further reinforce the concepts.

STORIES ●●●●●●●●●●●●●●●●●●●●●●●●●●●●●●●●●●●●●
AREA GOES 3-D

When your students are ready to calculate the area of three-dimensional shapes, you can extend the story of Area by sharing with your class the following brief update:

COMMON CORE STANDARDS

CCSS.Math.Content.3.MD.C.5

STORY

After several successful months working at the mattress store, Area's life changed forever when she went with her family one day to see her first 3-D movie. Walking out of the theater, she asked herself, "Why am I wasting my time lying down on flat things like rugs, hopscotch courts, and sleeping bags?" From that point on, Area began covering all the faces on cubes, prisms, pyramids, and other three-dimensional objects.

This update about Area's epiphany provides a way to understand the challenge of calculating the total area of three-dimensional objects. With cubes, for example, the kids can imagine Area lying down on each of the cube's six faces, determine the area of each face, and then add each part together.

FROM
STEVE'S CLASSROOM

To give students a hands-on experience with the concept of total area, we cover shoeboxes with graph paper that has one-inch by one-inch squares. Working in pairs, the kids calculate the total area of the shoeboxes using the squares on the graph paper to assist them.

STORIES ●
THE STORY OF VOLUME
(PRONOUNCED "VO • LOO • MAY")

This story introduces the geometric concept of volume, building on the Peri Meter and Area stories.

> **COMMON CORE STANDARDS**
>
> **CCSS.Math.Content.5.MD.C.3**

STORY

Unlike his neighbors Peri and Area, Volume has the unique ability to curl his body into a tight ball and completely fill the inside space of a three-dimensional shape. He can fit inside cubes, cones, spheres, prisms—anything. Volume touches the individual cubes (or cubic units) that comprise each 3-D shape. When Volume fills a shape, he is like someone doing a cannonball, tucking his legs up into a ball before splashing into the water.

PROCEDURE:

- Ask for a volunteer to be Volume. Hands will fly up. Before choosing someone, announce that this lucky person will get to stand up on the table and pretend to do a big cannonball onto the rug. The hands will now fly up with even greater fervor.

- Once the lucky student is chosen, have the volunteer sit on the edge of the desk for a brief orientation. Ask, "Are you ready to stand and attempt the cannonball?" When the child answers "Yes," ask, "Are you sure that you're ready?" Your volunteer will repeat, "Yes."

- Then break the bad news: "I'm just kidding, of course. It would be reckless and irresponsible to do let you a cannonball off the table onto the floor—how could you even suggest such a thing!"

It's great to make your kids laugh while they're learning.

STORIES ●●●●●●●●●●●●●●●●●●●●●●●●●●●●●●●● ●
THE FARMER'S MARKET

This story-plus-movement activity brings the coordinate grid to life and is a great way to introduce the concept.

PREPARATION:

- You'll need a classroom-sized grid. A rug made of carpet squares works well, or you can create a grid in your room with yarn, string, or painter's tape, or outdoors with sidewalk chalk.

- Put numbers on the bottom and the left side of the grid.

- Create cards that each have a picture of a fruit or vegetable on them, such as corn, broccoli, strawberries, peaches, etc.

- Place the fruit and vegetable cards at every intersection. Now the farmer's market is ready.

PROCEDURE:

- In this activity, students will practice the proper "across, then up" sequence of using ordered pairs by retrieving the fruits and vegetables that are placed at the various spots on the grid.

- Tell your class that today you are all going on a field trip to the farmer's market—a virtual trip right in the classroom.

STORY

- Choose the first student (Stella), who starts at point (0,0). Give her an ordered pair of numbers.

- To help her remember the proper "across, then up" order, the rest of the class calls out, "AU, Stella, remember to go across and then up on a coordinate grid." *AU* is a variation of the expression "Hey you," but the "A" stands for "across" and the "U" stands for "up." (With thanks to the old television show, "The Facts of Life.")

- Stella walks across and then up, stops at the ordered pair and announces the fruit or vegetable on the card located at that spot.

- As Stella moves across the grid, have her repeat both the numbers and the directions to strengthen the learning. For example, if you give Stella (2,5), she should call out "2 across" as she moves along the x-axis and "5 up" as she travels up the y-axis.

- If she is correct, collect her card, and Stella returns to her place. If she is incorrect, give her another try. Then the next student gets a turn.

- To provide additional practice, call out ordered pairs and have the kids respond with arm movements. For example, with (2, 5), all the kids would simultaneously chant "2 across" as they hold one arm parallel to the ground at chest level, then chant "5 up" as they hold that arm perpendicular.

By the conclusion of this activity, every child has received plenty of opportunities to see, hear, say, and move to the proper spot on the coordinate grid, reinforcing this concept.

FROM
STEVE'S CLASSROOM

A few student volunteers demonstrate this in a brief video on YouTube: www.youtube.com/watch?v=9LOw8IhDW7s

I like to promote healthy eating and exercise as often as I can, and using fruits and vegetables in The Farmer's Market reminds us all to eat more of what's good for us.

STORIES ●●●●●●●●●●●●●●●●●●●●●●●●●●●●●●●●●●●●●
AUTHENTIC MATH

Author Marilyn Burns has written extensively about how to help students develop better conceptual understanding.

From a book she co-wrote with Susan Ohanian entitled *Math By All Means: Division Grades 3-4*, an open-ended problem-solving activity is presented: children are asked to determine how

COMMON CORE STANDARDS

CCSS.Math.Content.3.OA.A.2
CCSS.Math.Content.3.OA.A.3

they would share $5.00 equally among four students. Burns and Ohanian offer this division problem in the context of an authentic, meaningful story to engage students on a deeper level and, as a result, increase their motivation to complete the task.

The story involves four students who find a $5.00 bill on the playground and turn it into the principal. He tells them that if nobody claims it, they can share the money if they can explain how to split the money equally. This task helps develop division skills and also reinforces the importance of honesty and cooperation, adding that extra layer of character and social skill development.

Another way to capitalize on the power of storytelling in the classroom is to incorporate the use of picture books into math instruction. Books such as *Anno's Mysterious Multiplying Jar, The Doorbell Rang,* and *17 Kings and 42 Elephants* are recommended by Burns to help students understand multiplication and division. Be on the lookout for other authentic situations, real-life examples, and picture books that offer windows into the math concepts you are teaching.

CHAPTER 3

TEACHING LANGUAGE ARTS WITH MOVEMENT AND STORIES

MOVEMENT

Classrooms can be sedentary places, and children can easily be sitting for long periods of time. Consequently, they will be grateful for any opportunity to stand, stretch, and move. If they're moving in ways that reflect or represent the concepts they are learning, so much the better.

FROM
STEVE'S CLASSROOM

Movement activities are easy to manage if clear instructions are provided. Be strict about the rules of each game, and ask students who are not following the rules to sit and watch. Make the point that even though they are fun and exciting, these games are classroom activities, and kids are expected to follow the rules, just as they are during more conventional lessons. I find that children are so excited to do these movement activities that behavior issues are rare.

MOVEMENT ●●●●●●●●●●●●●●●●●●●●●●●●●●●●●●●●
THE SYNONYM-ANTONYM SIDESTEP

This activity was inspired by Elly Goldman and
Denise Schiavone.

COMMON CORE STANDARDS

CCSS.ELA-Literacy.L.4.5c

PREPARATION:

- Before you do this activity with your
  class, prepare a set of approximately 20
  index cards with a word pair written on each—either synonyms or
  antonyms of each other. Possible synonym pairs could include *great-
  excellent* and *happy-cheerful*; possible antonym pairs could include
  up-down and *hot-cold*. See page 51 for synonym/antonym pair suggestions. Since the focus of this activity is on understanding the
  concept of synonyms and antonyms, not vocabulary, it's fine to use
  word pairs that may be easy for your students.

- Place the stack of index cards face down on the floor near the front wall.

PROCEDURE:

- The students stand in two lines, one on each side of the room,
  and face the center. The middle of the room needs to remain open
  because the kids will be moving through this area.

- The first person in each line walks to the pile of index cards and
  selects the top card. The other students slide up one place in line
  every time a new pair of students comes to the front to get a card.

- The two kids in the front of the room read the word pair aloud and
  decide if the words on their card are synonyms or antonyms. Then
  they return the card to the discard pile. If the words on the card are
  synonyms, the partners face each other, grab hands, and sidestep
  through the middle of the room to the end of their respective lines. If
  the words are antonyms, the kids stand back-to-back (facing opposite
  directions), grab hands, and sidestep through the center to the end of
  their lines. As the game progresses, the kids will associate the term
  synonym with the word *same* (because they're facing the same direction) and the term *antonym* with the word *opposite* (because they're
  facing the opposite direction). Repeat this idea throughout the game.

- To keep the children who are waiting in line engaged in the activity
  and to provide valuable reinforcement of these concepts, have everyone clap and chant either "syn-o-nym" or "ant-o-nym" each time a
  new pair of students sidesteps through the middle of the room.

SUGGESTED WORD PAIRS

SYNONYMS	ANTONYMS
happy-cheerful	up-down
rich-wealthy	hot-cold
smart-intelligent	optimistic-pessimistic
gigantic-large	clean-dirty
kind-nice	straight-crooked
tasty-delicious	sharp-dull
fantastic-wonderful	in-out
cruel-unkind	generous-selfish
hot-boiling	fast-slow
tiny-small	over-under

MOVEMENT ●●●●●●●●●●●●●●●●●●●●●●●●●●●●●●●●●●
THE JUMPING GAME

The Jumping Game helps reinforce the definition of synonyms and antonyms.

COMMON CORE STANDARDS

CCSS.ELA-Literacy.L.K.5b
CCSS.ELA-Literacy.L.4.5c

PREPARATION:

- Prepare a list of words for which your students can think of synonyms or antonyms.

PROCEDURE:

- Pair students and have them face their partners. They should stand a few feet away from their partners, with adequate space between each pair.

- The teacher announces the first word.

- The kids jump up and down on two feet twice, and then stick out one leg. It's like playing rock-paper-scissors with feet. To keep the kids jumping at the same speed as their partners, call out, "Jump, jump, show."

- If the partners show opposite legs, they think of as many antonyms as possible for the word and say them quietly to each other. If they show legs from the same side of their bodies, they brainstorm synonyms. **Example:** The word is *mean*. The kids jump once, jump twice, and show their feet. The pairs who show either two right feet or two left feet brainstorm synonyms, such as *cruel*, *rotten*, and *unkind*. The pairs that show one left and one right foot brainstorm antonyms, such as *friendly*, *kind*, and *nice*.

- Give the groups about 30 seconds to brainstorm their synonyms and antonyms, then bring everyone together for a quick whole class share. Check for accuracy, reinforce the meaning of the two terms, and compliment students who demonstrate excellent word choice.

Have your students do two to four words per session of the Jumping Game.

FROM
STEVE'S CLASSROOM

My student volunteers are demonstrating this game on YouTube:
www.youtube.com/watch?v=OF89SaxfHMc

MOVEMENT •••••••••••••••••••••••••••••••••
THE STORYTELLING CIRCLE

The Storytelling Circle is a simple strategy that helps students understand a wide variety of curricular concepts. In its basic form, children stand in a circle, think of examples of the topic at hand, and then take turns acting out those examples.

It works well for having students understand the definition of a verb.

> **COMMON CORE STANDARDS**
>
> **CCSS.ELA-Literacy.L.K.5d**
> **CCSS.ELA-Literacy.L.1.5d**
> **CCSS.ELA-Literacy.L.2.5b**

PROCEDURE:

- Give everyone a moment to think of a verb to share with the class.

- Then, standing in a circle, the first student says a verb and acts it out, reinforcing the idea that verbs usually show action.

- To promote attentive listening, either have the whole class repeat each student's verb and action before proceeding to the next person or have each student repeat the previous student's verb and action before doing his or her own.

The Storytelling Circle also works well with nouns and other language arts concepts that students can take turns demonstrating.

MOVEMENT ●●●●●●●●●●●●●●●●●●●●●●●●●●●●●●●
JUMP ROPES FOR ELA

Manuvering jump ropes into shapes helps kids understand a number of curricular concepts. When using jump ropes, yarn, or string to make letters and words, kids often pay more attention to detail and respond to your challenges with greater care and craftsmanship than they do when using paper and pencil.

COMMON CORE STANDARDS

CCSS.ELA-Literacy.RF.K.1d

PROCEDURE:

- Students lay out jump ropes (or long pieces of yarn or string) to form different printed and cursive letters or spelling words.

- Use this strategy any time you believe students would benefit from a break from paper-and-pencil activities in favor of a more kinesthetic approach.

Issuing challenges in an inquiry-based manner is the most effective way to use the jump ropes.

- If your students are learning to write in cursive, ask, "Can you form the lower case letter *s?*"

This strategy also works for numbers and shapes (see page 24).

MOVEMENT ●●●●●●●●●●●●●●●●●●●●●●●●●●●●●●●●●●●
INDEX CARD ARRANGING

Index Card Arranging helps kids understand a wide variety of concepts. The basic strategy is to have students arrange individual index cards into the correct sequence. This activity is appropriate for sequencing events of a story, placing words in alphabetical order, arranging words in a sentence with proper syntax, dividing the syllables in a word, assembling smaller words into compound words, working with prefix / base word / suffix combinations, reuniting words from the same word families, matching rhyming words, and categorizing items.

COMMON CORE STANDARDS

CCSS.ELA-Literacy.RF.2.3d
CCSS.ELA-Literacy.L.2.2e
CCSS.ELA-Literacy.L.2.4b
CCSS.ELA-Literacy.L.2.4c
CCSS.ELA-Literacy.RF.3.3a
CCSS.ELA-Literacy.RF.3.3b
CCSS.ELA-Literacy.L.3.2e
CCSS.ELA-Literacy.L.3.2g
CCSS.ELA-Literacy.L.4.4c
CCSS.ELA-Literacy.L.5.4c

EXAMPLE #1

Learning how to put words in alphabetical order

PREPARATION:

- Create a set of 10 to 20 large index cards with a different word written on each card.

PROCEDURE:

- Ask for five volunteers. (The more volunteers, the more complicated this activity becomes.)

- Give each volunteer a card and have them stand shoulder-to-shoulder and order themselves, displaying the cards in front of them so that the words are alphabetized from left to right.

- Once the kids have talked among themselves to solve this challenge, the rest of the class assesses the order and makes any necessary corrections.

Because this activity moves fairly quickly, you can accomplish quite a bit in only a few minutes and every child can have a turn.

VARIATION:

Divide your students into groups and give each a stack of index cards. All the groups can work through their challenges at once. After each group completes their challenge, come back together as a class to check for accuracy.

EXAMPLE #2

Learning prefix / base word / suffix combinations

PREPARATION:

- Create and laminate three sets of large index cards:
    - red cards with prefixes on the front and their meanings on the back
    - yellow cards with base words
    - blue cards with suffixes on the front and their meanings on the back

Maintain a list for your reference of all of these words

PROCEDURE:

- Give each student one or more cards and call out a word, such as *careful*. The child with the *care* card joins the one with the *ful* suffix card at the front of the room to form the word *careful*. Seeing the two parts of the word in different colors come together provides children with a visual and kinesthetic way to understand prefixes and suffixes.

It's fun to end each session of this activity with the "Randomizer." Call three kids at random—one who's holding a prefix, one with a base word, and one with a suffix—to bring their cards to the front of the room. They put their cards together to form (usually) a nonsense word. The kids LOVE seeing what these random word parts create, and there is something about the silliness of the idea that reinforces the meaning of all three parts of the word, and the idea that these parts together form a larger word.

MOVEMENT ●●●●●●●●●●●●●●●●●●●●●●●●●●●●●●●●●●
READING AROUND THE ROOM

Comprehension often suffers when children read too quickly or fail to follow punctuation. To address these issues, use this activity adapted from Marcia Tate's book, *Worksheets Don't Grow Dendrites*.

COMMON CORE STANDARDS

CCSS.ELA-Literacy.RF.1.4b
CCSS.ELA-Literacy.RF.2.4b
CCSS.ELA-Literacy.RF.3.4b
CCSS.ELA-Literacy.SL.3.5
CCSS.ELA-Literacy.RF.4.4b
CCSS.ELA-Literacy.RF.5.4b

PROCEDURE:

- Students stand in a large circle with a common text in their hands.

- On the "go" signal, everyone reads aloud, in unison, from a predetermined starting point.

- While reading, everyone slowly walks forward. At every comma, students stop walking and pause in their reading for one second before resuming their walking and reading. At every period, exclamation point, or question mark, the kids stop and pause in their reading for two seconds before resuming their walking and reading.

You may need to add other movements for additional punctuation in your reading selection. Reading and moving together provides a strong physical and vocal structure to help children who may struggle to follow these rules.

This activity helps everyone learn to read with better fluency, volume, and expression. Using Reading Around the Room only three minutes per day for a couple of weeks makes a huge difference in reading proficiency.

MOVEMENT ●●●●●●●●●●●●●●●●●●●●●●●●●●●●●●●●●
THE SLOUCH GAME

The Slouch Game helps students distinguish between proper nouns (which begin with capital letters because they name specific people, places, and things) and common nouns (which do not require capitals).

COMMON CORE STANDARDS

CCSS.ELA-Literacy.L.1.2a
CCSS.ELA-Literacy.L.2.2a
CCSS.ELA-Literacy.L.3.2a
CCSS.ELA-Literacy.L.4.2a

PROCEDURE:

- The game begins with everyone seated in chairs. Call out a noun. If it is a proper noun, the kids sit up tall in their chairs to approximate the height of a capital letter. If it is a common noun, the kids slouch to approximate the height of a lower case letter. Kids love the novelty of this game because teachers and parents are constantly telling them to sit up straight, but now they are required to slouch as part of the game!

- In the beginning of the activity, alternate between common nouns and their corresponding proper nouns in order to establish an easy-to-follow pattern, build student confidence, and give the kids a nice mini-workout. For example, you could start with the following words: *city* (slouch), *Los Angeles* (sit tall), *school* (slouch), *Roosevelt School* (sit tall), *team* (slouch), *Dodgers* (sit tall).

- Once you have established a pattern, break it so the students must listen and think more carefully. Call out common or proper nouns at random. You can quickly assess which students need more follow-up with these concepts.

Children who struggle with differentiating these types of nouns are able to correct their mistakes easily, since they can look around and observe what the other students are doing. The Slouch Game can also be used to help students learn other capitalization rules.

FROM
STEVE'S CLASSROOM

A YouTube video of my student volunteers demonstrating the game: www.youtube.com/watch?v=jJsGw3eI0S4

MOVEMENT ●●●●●●●●●●●●●●●●●●●●●●●●●●●●●●●●●●●
READING COMPREHENSION DRIBBLING

To improve reading comprehension, students are expected to learn the strategies of predicting, monitoring, questioning, and summarizing. Reading Comprehension Dribbling helps students practice the order and timing of these four strategies.

Many students find it hard to remember to use these strategies at the appropriate times: making a prediction about a text *before* they start reading, monitoring their understanding and asking questions about the text *as* they are reading, and summarizing the key points of the text *after* they have finished reading.

COMMON CORE STANDARDS

CCSS.ELA-Literacy.RF.1.4a
CCSS.ELA-Literacy.RF.2.4a
CCSS.ELA-Literacy.RF.3.4a
CCSS.ELA-Literacy.RF.4.4a
CCSS.ELA-Literacy.RF.5.4a

PREPARATION:

- Go to a basketball court or other playground rectangle. You can also do this in your classroom by creating court-like boundaries on your rug or floor.

PROCEDURE:

- Students stand at the baseline with a ball in their hands. If there aren't enough balls for each child to have one, you may need to form a few lines, but emphasize that this is not a relay race or competition of any kind. If the kids' desire to race becomes an issue, start the first person in each line at different times.

- Before taking the first dribble, everyone yells, "predict!" Predicting before dribbling reinforces the idea that we predict before we begin reading. Then everyone starts dribbling to the other end line. While dribbling, the kids repeat the words "question" and "monitor" to reinforce the idea that active readers ask questions and monitor their understanding as they read. After arriving at the opposite baseline, the kids hold the ball and yell, "summarize!"

Practicing the strategies in motion on a basketball court and viewing them as a "journey through a book" provides students with a structure and reference point they can use as they turn these strategies into lifetime habits.

MOVEMENT ●●●●●●●●●●●●●●●●●●●●●●●●●●●●●●●●●●● CARD SORT

Card Sort is a logical thinking strategy that can be used whenever children need to divide information into categories or demonstrate understanding of specific rules.

A good use of the Card Sort technique is for teaching the four types of sentences—statement, command, exclamation, and question.

COMMON CORE STANDARDS

CCSS.ELA-Literacy.L.1.1j
CCSS.ELA-Literacy.L.1.2a
CCSS.ELA-Literacy.L.2.2a
CCSS.ELA-Literacy.L.3.2a
CCSS.ELA-Literacy.L.4.2a

PREPARATION:

- Write 15 to 20 of each type of sentence on index cards (one short sentence to a card).

- Label one shoebox for each sentence type—statement, command, exclamation, and question—and place one shoebox in each corner of the room.

- Put the sentence cards in the center of the room.

PROCEDURE:

- Students take turns picking a sentence card and placing it in the appropriate shoebox.

VARIATIONS:

There are several opportunities for differentiation in the way you conduct the activity:

- Have the students sort in pairs to make the activity more social and increase the likelihood of correct placement.

- Designate one highly proficient student to be the "go to" person in case any participants need assistance placing their cards.

- Station a highly proficient student at each box to serve as a gatekeeper. Before placing a given card in a given box, students check with the gatekeeper, who either graciously accepts the placement or kindly suggests that the sorter head in a different direction.

- Incorporating specific movements into the sorting process adds an additional dimension. Before a student places a card into a box, have that person do a movement associated with the type of sentence on the card. Establish these movements in advance. For example, have students shrug the shoulders to show that the sentence type is a question, or flash a big smile to indicate an exclamation. Attaching a movement helps reinforce the concepts, and also enables the teacher to assess quickly how students are faring.

However you choose to structure the activity, a short period of whole class debriefing should follow. Go through each box, acknowledge correct placements, and make any necessary corrections. Many mistakes indicate the need for additional instruction.

Card sorting works well with capitalization rules, food groups, and key words that indicate which operation students may want to use to solve math word problems (e.g., "How many does he *have left?*" would go in the subtraction box).

MOVEMENT ●●●●●●●●●●●●●●●●●●●●●●●●●●●●●●●●●●
THE CONTRACTION BLUES

The Contraction Blues is a whole-class letter game to help students learn about contractions. The game helps students understand that when two words are contracted, one or more letters are taken away, and the resulting word is shorter than the two original words.

> **COMMON CORE STANDARDS**
>
> **CCSS.ELA-Literacy.L.2.2c**

PREPARATION:

- Make one set of individual letter cards using large index cards. Laminate them if possible. If you have more than 26 students, prepare extra cards for the common letters (such as *n, l, t,* and *e*).

- For your reference, prepare a list of words your students are learning to contract.

PROCEDURE:

- Give each student in class a letter card.

- Start by calling out the first words to contract—*is* and *not*, for example. The students with those letters come to the front of the room, hold their cards in front of them for the class to see, and stand shoulder to shoulder to spell out the words, leaving a space between the words.

- Choose a volunteer to be the Contractor. The Contractor determines which unlucky cardholder needs to sit back down because he/she is in possession of the letter *o*, which is dropped when *is* and *not* contract to form *isn't,* and escorts that now unnecessary person off the stage. Naturally, kids love being the Contractor. They love tapping someone on the shoulder and politely informing the person that his/her services are, for the time being, no longer required.

- The holder of the *o* then sadly returns to his/her spot. Keep tissues nearby to help the exiting student deal with the emotional pain of being contracted and cope with "the Contraction Blues." Let the kids ham it up.

- Once that unpleasantness is over, the Contractor steps in between the *n* and the *t* and forms an apostrophe with his/her hand while the holders of the *i* and the *s* move closer to the others to eliminate the space that separates the two words. This physical shortening is crucial. The class has a chance to see the contracted word *isn't* with the apostrophe in the right place and with the resulting contraction physically shorter than the two words that made it. Remind students that the word is now shorter so they understand the meaning of the word *contraction*.

- Proceed through a few more examples so more children can have a turn and the kids can see this shortening principle reinforced. Start with simple examples such as *I'm* and *wasn't* and then proceed to more complicated contractions, such as *she'll* and *won't*. To prevent the students holding letters such as *x* or *q* from being left out, ask them to serve as Contractors.

FROM
STEVE'S CLASSROOM

Many kids struggle with contractions because they either put the apostrophe in the wrong place or omit it entirely. As a preface to this game, introduce the word "contract" and emphasize that when something contracts it gets smaller or shorter. To demonstrate this concept, find a student wearing short sleeves, call him/her to the front of the room, and have the student extend his/her arm straight out. With your fingers, measure the length of the student's arm from the shoulder to the elbow. Ask the student to flex the bicep. Most kids will look to see the height of the muscle, but you should focus on how the contraction of the bicep makes the length of the muscle shorter, and emphasize that when something contracts, it gets shorter.

STORIES

In the classroom, teachers can use the engaging power of stories to help students learn a wide variety of academic content. When teaching content that is somewhat abstract, consider whether there is a way to teach the concept using storytelling. Can you create interesting characters or outlandish storylines that will hook kids, feature the content children are expected to learn, and bring that content to life in a way that will entertain the class and help everyone remember the information for a long time to come? That's the goal of a story.

STORIES ●●●●●●●●●●●●●●●●●●●●●●●●●●●●●●●●●●●●
THE TRIP TO THE ZOO

This movement story helps students understand the rules for using apostrophes to show possession.

COMMON CORE STANDARDS

CCSS.ELA-Literacy.L.2.2c
CCSS.ELA-Literacy.L.3.2d

PREPARATION:

- Create two hand signals with your class —one to show 's and one to show s'.

- One method for hand signals: students hold both hands in front of their faces. Turn the left hand into an apostrophe and the right into an s shape to signal 's and turn the left hand into an s and the right hand into an apostrophe to signal s'. (Even though there really isn't a way to bend a finger into an s shape, ask the kids to do it anyway. They will do it with confidence.)

- Another method is for each child to create two small signs—one with s' and one with 's—to hold up. Using both sides of a dry-erase board works well for these signs.

- Students may also work in pairs with one child in charge of signaling 's and the other responsible for displaying the s' sign. When the kids work in pairs, they make decisions together and students who struggle with this concept benefit from the support provided by classmates more proficient with this skill.

PROCEDURE:

- Read "The Trip to the Zoo" story to your students. Instruct them to respond with the signals as they listen.

- When the kids hear singular nouns that require 's to indicate possession, they flash the hand signal or hold up the sign for 's. When they hear plural nouns that require only an apostrophe, they flash or hold up the s' sign.

Keep a close eye on your students so you know which ones need further practice with these concepts. After you read the story aloud, you can remove the apostrophes (page 68). Display the story with no punctuation on a whiteboard and insert the apostrophes along the way, or give it to your students as a follow-up exercise.

STORY

Today was a big day for five-year old Reggie. For his birthday, his parents were taking him to the city zoo for the first time. As the family approached the entrance, Reggie absolutely couldn't wait to see the lions, giraffes, elephants, and other creatures he had heard so much about.

The first animal Reggie visited was the **zoo's** only tiger. Reggie wanted to stand right next to the fence for a clear look at the **tiger's** teeth, but in his **parents'** minds, that was too close to the cage for young Reggie. So, they quickly pulled him back by their **son's** hand. Reggie was disappointed by his **parents'** decision, but he moved to the next area with a smile.

A few seconds later, Reggie heard the loud roar of three lions. The **lions'** roars startled his Mom and Dad, but not Reggie. He kept smiling right up to the **lions'** cage. Once again his parents had to control **Reggie's** enthusiasm and pull him back.

After about an hour of visiting all the animals, **Reggie's** parents were pooped. They were ready to head home for a nap. His **parents'** energy level was simply no match for that of their young son. In fact, Reggie drove his sleepy parents home in the **family's** car.

FROM STEVE'S CLASSROOM

Once I wanted to use a movement-based activity that would help the kids differentiate between homophones. I gave each group of my students a common homophone pair and asked the students to create a way, using movement, to remember the meanings and spellings of each word in their pair.

They came up with great ideas. One group, for example, wrote the letter *h* on a piece of paper and held the sheet to their ears to show how *h* plus *ear* spells *hear*. Their demonstration helped classmates distinguish *hear* from *here*. Another pair of students used invisible shovels to pretend to dig the letter *w* out of the ground to distinguish *hole* from *whole* (as if to announce that there's no *w* in the word *hole*). The kids were able to piggyback on one another's ideas, and everyone came away with a better understanding and greater awareness of the subtle differences found in many common homophones.

We teachers often think that we have to create all the teaching strategies we use. But when you involve the kids, two great things happen: the students come up with incredibly clever ideas, and they really appreciate the opportunity to make suggestions, which builds a greater sense of connection to school and a greater sense of ownership of what happens in the classroom.

THE TRIP TO THE ZOO (NO PUNCTUATION)

Today was a big day for five-year old Reggie. For his birthday, his parents were taking him to the city zoo for the first time. As the family approached the entrance, Reggie absolutely couldn't wait to see the lions, giraffes, elephants, and other creatures he had heard so much about.

The first animal Reggie visited was the **zoos** only tiger. Reggie wanted to stand right next to the fence for a clear look at the **tigers** teeth, but in his **parents** minds, that was too close to the cage for young Reggie. So, they quickly pulled him back by their **sons** hand. Reggie was disappointed by his **parents** decision, but he moved to the next area with a smile.

A few seconds later, Reggie heard the loud roar of three lions. The **lions** roars startled his Mom and Dad, but not Reggie. He kept smiling right up to the **lions** cage. Once again his parents had to control **Reggies** enthusiasm and pull him back.

After about an hour of visiting all the animals, **Reggies** parents were pooped. They were ready to head home for a nap. His **parents** energy level was simply no match for that of their young son. In fact, Reggie drove his sleepy parents home in the **familys** car.

CHAPTER 4

TEACHING SCIENCE, SOCIAL STUDIES, AND HEALTH WITH MOVEMENT AND STORIES

MOVEMENT AND STORIES

Activities that incorporate movement and stories work well across the whole curriculum. The concepts in science, social studies, and health can be complicated or abstract, so finding new ways to explain these topics can help our students understand them. The stories in this chapter also have a movement component to improve student understanding. Some of these movement activities can be coordinated with what the students are doing in their physical education class.

SCIENCE ●●●●●●●●●●●●●●●●●●●●●●●●●●●●●●●●●●●●
SOLID, LIQUID, AND GAS

This activity helps students learn the three states of matter (solids, liquids, and gases) and how molecules behave in those states.

PROCEDURE:

- Begin by having your kids spread out in the classroom with each child at least an arm's distance away from the nearest classmate.

- Announce that the temperature is a comfortable 65 degrees Fahrenheit. The kids start as liquid water, doing a slow jog in place and maintaining their arm's distance separation. This simulates the concept that molecules in a liquid move at a moderate speed and are neither very close nor far away from other molecules. This activity can also be done using the Celsius scale.

- Announce that the temperature is dropping all the way down to 32 degrees Fahrenheit, and as a result, the water is freezing. Students now slow their jogging almost to a complete stop and move toward the center in a room in a tight cluster. Challenge your students to get as close as they can to one another without touching. Slowing down and huddling together reinforces the idea that molecules in a solid (ice) move very slowly and have little distance between them.

- Announce that the temperature has just risen to 65 degrees Fahrenheit, and the kids return to their liquid formation.

- Announce that the temperature has just increased to 212 degrees Fahrenheit. Now the kids should jog in place at close to breakneck speed and spread out in the room to the greatest extent possible without knocking into walls. They now represent gas molecules. Running in place reminds the students of walking on hot sand, and the idea of hot feet helps them remember the fact that they are extremely "hot" molecules.

FROM
STEVE'S CLASSROOM

The Solid, Liquid, and Gas activity works well with the "Human Thermometer" chant in Chapter 7 (page 152).

- Now call out random temperatures. The students should respond by adjusting their jogging-in-place speeds and their relative distances to one another.

While they transition from one "state" to another, you can assess quickly which students may benefit from additional follow-up.

SCIENCE ●●●●●●●●●●●●●●●●●●●●●●●●●●●●●●
STATES of MATTER

These two stories address the three states of matter (solid, liquid, and gas) and the changes that can occur among them (melting, freezing, boiling, evaporating, condensing). The first, "The Story of Tammy and Tommy," incorporates these scientific terms using their literal meanings. The story works well to introduce or review these concepts. The second story, "Going for the Gold," features non-literal use of these terms and, because the words are used in completely different ways, works well as an assessment of student proficiency.

The following movements apply to both stories. Students perform the movements when they hear the corresponding word as the teacher reads the story aloud. This type of movement story also reinforces listening skills.

Solid	clasp hands together, interweaving fingers (clasp)
Liquid	put one hand on top of the other in the shape of a glass (glass)
Gas	hands start together, then separate like a starburst (starburst)
Freeze	glass to clasp slowly (because molecules are slowing down)
Melt	clasp to glass quickly (because molecules are speeding up)
Evaporate	glass to starburst quickly (because molecules are speeding up)
Boil	glass to starburst even more quickly (because molecules are really speeding up)
Condense	starburst to glass slowly (because molecules are slowing down)

THE STORY OF TAMMY AND TOMMY

Once there was a boy named Tommy, who lived in the warm climate of Florida. His older sister Tammy was away at college in the cold climate of Wisconsin. The two siblings would often do similar activities, but they would turn out differently because of the different climates.

Tommy bought a Popsicle, a **solid**. When he took it outside, the **solid** quickly **melted** into water, a **liquid**. Tommy was very disappointed. That same day, Tammy poured herself a nice glass of juice, a **liquid**. When she took it outside, it quickly **froze** into a **solid**. She was even more disappointed.

One fall afternoon, Tommy and Tammy both decided to go swimming after school. For Tommy, this was no big deal. Warm, sunny days happened all the time in Florida. But for Tammy, a warm sunny day in November was a special treat. To celebrate the occasion, she bought a pink balloon, filled it with air (a **gas**), and tied the balloon's string to a nearby lounge chair before entering the water, a **liquid**.

Tommy swam for a while in the **liquid** pool and then relaxed in his lounge chair. A short time later, his bathing suit was dry. Most of the water had **evaporated** into a **gas**. Tommy, however, was someone who liked his bathing suit completely dry, so he asked his mom to **boil** it on the stove. She refused.

Tammy, on the other hand, didn't have such a pleasant experience. Just as she was about to dive into the water, a **liquid**, a huge gust of wind came out of nowhere, and the temperature dropped tremendously. The **gas** in her balloon suddenly **condensed** into water, a **liquid**, and started dripping out of the balloon. Going for a swim wasn't such a good idea anymore. Tammy was so upset she decided to move back home immediately.

GOING FOR THE GOLD

Today was a big day for Dane. He had been training to win the city swimming championship for a whole year, and today was the day. Though there were going to be many other fine swimmers at the meet, Dane thought that only Jeremy had a chance to beat him. Jeremy had beaten Dane the last five times they competed against each other, and Dane knew he would have to be at his best to capture the gold medal.

When Dane arrived at the pool, he felt confident. He thought his chances for a gold medal were **solid**. After drinking some **liquid** and stretching for a few minutes, Dane looked around and noticed something. Jeremy was nowhere to be found. "Maybe Jeremy's car ran out of **gas**," he hoped to himself. Just then, the announcer called all the swimmers to the starting blocks. Once all the swimmers were in position, Dane looked around him again. Still no sign of Jeremy.

Then, just as the starting horn was about to sound, Dane heard a door open. It was Jeremy. Seeing his rival at the last minute like this really made Dane's blood **boil**. He could feel his hopes **evaporating**. He could sense his chance for a victory and a gold medal **melting** away. Jeremy quickly made his way to the starting block, and the race was now only seconds away from beginning.

Out of nowhere, Dane felt something change inside of him. He was no longer afraid of Jeremy. Dane turned toward Jeremy, his eyes **frozen** on his competitor. Dane became very determined. He took all the ideas flying through his mind and **condensed** them into one single thought: nothing is going to stop me today. Dane turned his head, and now his eyes were **frozen** on the **liquid** in front of him.

The horn sounded, and Dane exploded out of the blocks. This was just the type of **solid** start he needed in order to **melt** away his fears. Dane built a big lead over Jeremy, and a minute later, it was over. Dane was the champion!

⬤ SCIENCE ●●●●●●●●●●●●●●●●●●●●●●●●●●●●●●●●●●
RAINFOREST LAYERS

This story familiarizes students with the main parts of the rainforest by taking them on a virtual tour. In addition, the story incorporates key scientific concepts, such as how plants and animals depend on one another to live and how the bodies of various creatures often possess survival features that enable them to avoid predators, capture prey, and take advantage of their surrounding environment.

PROCEDURE:

- Have your students stand and act out the highlighted verbs as they listen to the story.

STORY OF THE RAINFOREST

You are a large crocodile **swimming** in one of the rainforest's winding rivers **searching** for your lunch. **Blink** your three eyelids that protect your eyes as you **swim**. **Push hard** through the water using your powerful, flexible tail. **Chomp down** with your mighty jaws that carry over 60 teeth.

You are now a tiny insect **crawling** around on the forest floor. **Snack** on the many dead leaves that cover the forest floor. **Watch out**, though, for the anteaters coming after you.

You are now a green tree frog **hopping** on a leafy bromeliad in the rainforest's second layer, the understory. **Hide** in the leaves whose green color nicely camouflages your green skin. **Take a nap** during these hot daylight hours to save on water loss. **Soak up** the falling rainwater that these bromeliads catch.

You are now a tree **swaying in** the wind in the rainforest's third layer, the canopy. **Flex** your muscles to show off your thick branches. **Smile** as you enjoy checking out all the different creatures that live in this area. More wildlife lives here than anywhere else. **Turn your palms up and catch** the falling rain, keeping most of it from reaching the forest floor below.

You are now an athletic monkey **flying** high on our final stop, the emergent layer. **Swing** from tree to tree, but don't look down. You're about 200 feet in the air. **Stay alert** at all times! The eagle has its eyes on you!

SCIENCE ●●●●●●●●●●●●●●●●●●●●●●●●●●●●●●●●●●
SOURCES OF ENERGY CHALLENGE

This activity helps students learn about the various sources of energy used in the world. Although it is possible to play this game inside the classroom, it works best in an outdoor space.

PREPARATION:

- Establish two end lines about 20 to 30 feet apart. If your playground has a basketball or volleyball court with the lines already made, use those, even if the distance is a bit off. Feel free to adjust the distance based on the age of your students.

- Prepare playground balls to represent the sources of energy. You'll need at least one ball for every pair of students. Tennis balls can work if you're lacking other equipment, but bigger balls such as basketballs, kick balls, and soccer balls generally work better for this activity.

- Label each ball to represent one of the four different energy sources—the sun, batteries, gasoline, and food. You can write directly on the ball with marker or write the term on an index card and tape it to the ball. You'll need several of each type of energy source.

- Place the "balls of energy" along the far baseline.

PROCEDURE:

- Teams of two students line up along the baseline opposite the balls. Designate each pair to represent a different "energy user," a living creature or inanimate object that requires energy in order to live or work. For example, one pair may be a computer, another pair a car, a plant, a dog, or a toy.

- The students pretend that they are almost completely out of energy. In order to find some, the pairs stand shoulder-to-shoulder and drag themselves listlessly to the baseline with the balls.

- When a pair reaches the baseline, the two kids pick up the type of energy they require (e.g., a computer picks up a battery), place it between their hips, and start walking with it.

- To complete the challenge, a pair must walk to the original baseline, touch it with their feet, and return to the line where the energy was found. If the ball drops at any point along the way, the pair must return to the baseline where they picked up their energy and begin again.

Children learn quickly that they will be successful only by working cooperatively with their partners. Pairs that successfully arrive at the finish line may do a short energy dance before putting the ball down and running back to the starting point. If there's time, the pair may attempt the challenge a second time as a different energy user.

SCIENCE ●●●●●●●●●●●●●●●●●●●●●●●●●●●●●●●●●●●
THE ENERGY WAVE

This activity helps demonstrate the way energy moves in a wave, and it's also great for team building in your class. Thanks to Project Adventure for inspiring the Energy Wave.

PREPARATION:

- There are two ways to do the Energy Wave. For the method that requires more preparation, you'll need PVC piping. Get the piping cut into four-foot-long sections, and then each section cut in half lengthwise. The students work in groups of four to six. Each student can have his/her own piece of pipe, or you can have half the number of pipes as students, to encourage sharing. You also need one golf ball or marble for every group of students.

- For simpler preparation, you'll need one ball or ruler for each group of four to six kids.

PROCEDURE:

Using PVC pipes:

- The kids line up with their pipe halves end-to-end.

- The first student rolls a golf ball down his/her pipe to the beginning of the next person's pipe, and the rolling continues from pipe to pipe. The moving ball represents energy as it travels in a sound wave, light wave, or other type of wave.

- After passing the golf ball, the first student then runs ahead and goes to the end of the line so there is always a student in place to receive the golf ball from the previous student. This chain reaction continues until the ball travels to the end of the field.

- If the ball hits the ground, the team continues from the point where the ball dropped.

Using balls or rulers:

- The kids can pass a ball or ruler from child to child from one end of the field to another. The ball or ruler represents the energy, and the kids' arms represent the energy wave.

VARIATION:

- Depending on the age of your students, you might want to use a marble instead of a golf ball with the PVC pipes to facilitate student success.

SCIENCE ●●●●●●●●●●●●●●●●●●●●●●●●●●●●●
WAXING AND WANING

This story helps students learn the difference between two important vocabulary terms pertaining to the lunar cycle, *wax* and *wane*. When the moon *waxes,* it appears to grow in brightness and roundness. When it *wanes*, the opposite is true, and the moon appears to lessen in brightness and roundness.

PROCEDURE:

- Read the story to your students.

- Instruct them to use the following hand movements when they hear the words *wax* and *wane* as they listen:

   Wax *(visible part of moon increases)*
   touch the fingertips of both hands together and then separate the hands to about a foot apart.

   Wane *(visible part of moon decreases)*
   start with the fingertips about a foot apart and then bring the hands together until all corresponding fingers are touching.

STORY

Rodney needed to go to sleep soon, but he still hadn't studied for his astronomy quiz the next morning. He was pretty comfortable with all the material, but he still kept getting confused by the terms **wax** and **wane**. He just couldn't remember that when the moon **waxes**, it grows in brightness and roundness, and when it **wanes**, it decreases in brightness and roundness.

He thought it would be a good idea to find someone to help him study, but every member of his family seemed to be too busy to help him. Rodney's brother Kyle was busy **waxing** his surfboard. His father couldn't help because he was too focused on the **waning** minutes of the football game on TV. His sister Tina was down in the garage **waxing** her car. Rodney's hopes of finding a study partner began to **wane**. There was just one person left to ask, dear old Mom. Unfortunately, Mom was on the phone with her aunt, **waxing** poetically about the good old days they spent growing up back on the farm in Iowa.

Just as Rodney's hopes were about to **wane** completely, the football game ended, and Dad was able to help Rodney master these terms and ace his quiz the next day.

SCIENCE ●●●●●●●●●●●●●●●●●●●●●●●●●●●●●●
SPACE JAM

Space Jam increases students' familiarity with the planets while taking them on a virtual tour of our solar system. This story was developed by the Activity Promotion Laboratory of East Carolina University.

PROCEDURE:

- Read the following story aloud.

- Have students act out the highlighted verbs as they listen.

STORY

Hello, my name is Zippy and I live on a space station. Today I will lead you on a tour through space. First, we need to **put on** our moon boots. They will allow us to **walk** through space.

The first stop will be Mercury, the closest planet to the sun. Mercury is very hot, so—OUCH—be careful and **step quickly** so your feet do not get burned. Mercury also has many craters. On the count of three, let's **jump** into a crater and see what we find. One, two, three, JUMP!

Climb out of the crater so we can **march** to Venus. Venus is the second planet from the sun. This planet has very strong winds and volcanoes. See if you can **walk** through the wind without **blowing over**. A lot of the surface of Venus is covered with lava, and here comes some—RUN!

The next stop is Earth, the third planet from the sun. Seventy-one percent of the Earth's surface is water, so **hop in** and start **swimming**. See if you can do the **front crawl** and the **backstroke**.

Our next stop will be Mars. Mars is known as the red planet. The largest mountain in space, Olympic Mons, is located on Mars. See if you can **climb** to the top!

Jupiter is the fifth planet from the sun. It is made up of mostly gas and you can see clouds when you look at this planet. **Find a cloud** and see if you can **float** on it.

Our next stop is Saturn, the sixth planet from the sun. It has a rocky core and there are areas of ice throughout the planet. There are also rings of gases around Saturn. WHOA—there is a huge piece of ice! Be careful and **slide** across it. **Hop** on one of the rings surrounding Saturn and **spin around** in circles.

Uranus is our next stop. It has a small rocky core. Can everyone **tiptoe** across Uranus watching out for the ice?

Next, let's visit Neptune. Neptune has four rings and large storms with fast winds. It also has 13 moons. Quick, **duck!** Here comes a moon! **Move to the left** so you do not get hit. This ends our tour of space. **Grab** a partner and **hop** back to the space station.

SCIENCE ●●●●●●●●●●●●●●●●●●●●●●●●●●●●●●●●●●●
ROTATING AND REVOLVING

Kids frequently have difficulty distinguishing the term *rotate* (which the earth does on its axis daily) from the term *revolve* (which it does once around the sun each year). This activity provides children with an opportunity to act out the meaning of these concepts to gain greater clarity.

PREPARATION:

- Enlist the help of one bright student volunteer to be the sun. That child basically stands in the middle of the classroom or outdoor space looking cheerful and spreading light to everyone.

- Ask for another student volunteer to represent the earth.

PROCEDURE:

- Standing in place, the earth-child spins around slowly while saying "rotate."

- Now ask the child to stop rotating and start walking a lap around the sun. While doing so, the child repeats the word "revolve."

- Now, here's the hard part. Ask the earth-child to rotate and revolve around the sun at the same time while repeating both words.

- Have all the students form pairs and spread out.

- One student in each pair begins as the shining sun, while the other student in the pair assumes the role of earth.

- Call out "rotate," and all the earth-kids should turn on their respective axes and repeat the word "rotate."

- Do the same with "revolve."

- Bring it all together and have them rotate and revolve simultaneously.

- Switch roles so the earths can be the suns and the suns can be the earths.

VARIATIONS:

- If you're feeling ambitious, you can attempt to have all eight planets rotate and revolve around the sun at the same time. Use an outdoor area for this, or you're just asking for a collision!

- You can have the planets spread out equally or according to their actual relative distances from the sun.

- You can add moons and other space objects. If you try this, do it in two shifts. That way, everyone has a chance to participate and a chance to watch, and students may learn more by watching than by doing because they will be able to focus on the bigger picture.

SCIENCE ●●●●●●●●●●●●●●●●●●●●●●●●●●●●●●●●
THE WATER CYCLE

You can use your playground equipment to help your students learn some science terms. Rachel O'Donnell, a first grade teacher in Bahrain who teaches second-language learners, uses this activity to reinforce the water cycle.

PREPARATION:

- Go out to the playground.

- The teacher is the sun. It's fun if you wear a big sun hat!

- All the students are water droplets in the ocean.

PROCEDURE:

- As the "sun" taps a student's head, the student shouts, "evaporation!" and climbs up the jungle gym.

- At the top the student shouts, "condensation!"

- Once there are six students huddled in a group at the top of the jungle gym, they move to the slide and shout, "precipitation!" as they slide down the slide one at a time.

- When landing back in the "ocean" (on the ground), they shout, "collection!"

- The "sun" touches other students, and the water cycle continues.

SCIENCE ●●●●●●●●●●●●●●●●●●●●●●●●●●●●●
THE LIFE CYCLE OF A BUTTERFLY

Physical education teacher Mary Hirt uses a variation of the classic game Rock-Paper-Scissors to help kids learn about animal life cycles. The students gradually adjust the heights of their bodies to show the various stages of animal development. In this example we're focusing on the life cycle of a butterfly.

PREPARATION:

- Pair up students any way you choose.

PROCEDURE:

- Students begin the game as eggs by squatting as low as possible on the floor.
- They play "Rock-Paper-Scissors," and the winner of each showdown rises part way to simulate a caterpillar.
- Those who do not win find another egg and face off for the chance to become a caterpillar.
- Each pair of caterpillars then vies to become a chrysalis, who grows a little taller.
- Pairs of chrysalises face off to become butterflies.
- After two butterflies square off, the winner returns to the beginning and becomes an egg again.

This game can be used to demonstrate other examples of animal growth and body development.

SOCIAL STUDIES ●●●●●●●●●●●●●●●●●●●●●●●●●●●●●●●
ON the MAP

This activity comes from Dave Blackney, a physical education teacher in Anaheim, California. You can use it to help students identify physical features on a map or the location of all fifty states of the United States.

PREPARATION:

- Find a map that shows ten to fifteen unlabeled physical features. A typical social studies text will have this type of map. If you're using this activity for identifying states, you'll need an unlabeled map of the United States.

- Photocopy one map for each pair of students.

- Use a running track, either a real one on your playground or one you set up with cones. Make the size work for the age of your students.

- Label Popsicle sticks with the names of the physical features or states on your map. Prepare about three sticks for each feature or state.

- Each pair of students works together to label each feature or state correctly on their map. Each pair establishes a home base in a different location around the track.

- Place a box of Popsicle sticks at another spot near the track.

PROCEDURE:

- On the "go" signal, one member of each pair jogs around the track, stops at the box, and picks a stick without looking at it.

- The runners continue their laps until they return to their respective home bases, where they read the word printed on their sticks and write it on the correct physical feature or state on the sheet. (If students haven't yet mastered this material, you may want to set up a "reference center" off to the side of the track for them to visit when necessary. You can place a textbook in this area or a completed sheet.)

- Once the first member of each pair has returned home with a stick, the second member takes off and does the same thing.

- The members of each pair continue taking turns retrieving sticks and labeling the features on the sheets.

- Every time they do a lap, students drop their old sticks into the box before taking their new ones.

- Having one student from each pair always remain at home base prevents too many people from being at the box at the same time and ensures that the papers and pencils don't blow away. During that moment when one person is returning home and before the other partner has taken off for the next stick, the kids work together to identify the feature and write it on their map.

- The kids keep running until they have filled in all the blanks on their papers or until time elapses.

- If a child grabs a stick showing a word that has already been added to the pair's sheet, he/she may not put it back (they aren't supposed to look at the stick until they get back to home base). Instead, he/she finishes the lap, returns to his/her partner, finds that they have already identified that one, and the partner takes off for the next stick.

Review all the correct answers with your students at the conclusion of the activity, outside or back in class.

SOCIAL STUDIES ●●●●●●●●●●●●●●●●●●●●●●●●●●●
IMPORTING AND EXPORTING

This game, inspired by Dave Blackney, is a variation of the playground classic, Steal the Bacon. In this version, rather than competing, the two teams cooperate to illustrate the concepts of importing and exporting.

PREPARATION:

- Find a basketball court or a grass field to play this game.

- Prepare a few dozen products—index cards with the name of a good written on it, such as a computer, automobile, corn, or shoes.

- Divide your kids into two teams, with each team representing a different country. A midline divides the court in half. One side of the court represents Country A, and the other side represents Country B.

- Place the product cards near each end line of the field. If you're playing on a basketball court, place them in the two keys of the court.

The object of the game is for Country A to import goods from Country B while its own goods are being exported to Country B, and vice versa.

PROCEDURE:

- Each team starts the game in their own country, on opposite sides of the midline. Within their teams, some kids choose to be "importers" and others play defense and will tag the importers from the other country.

- On the "go" signal, kids who are "importers" try to cross through the other country's territory, grab one of the cards, and bring it back to their home country without getting tagged.

- If they make it back to their home country, they hand the card to the teacher, who adds it to the team's total.

- Players who are tagged must return the goods, return to their sides, and try again.

This game focuses on importing, but emphasize to your students that in real life, both importing and exporting are essential parts of our economy.

SOCIAL STUDIES ●●●●●●●●●●●●●●●●●●●●●●●●●●●●●●●
RUN ACROSS AMERICA

This activity combines map skills with movement. Although it is called "Run Across America," you can start anywhere in the world and travel to any destination you wish. Perhaps you want to travel from your hometown of Santa Fe, New Mexico to Washington, DC for the next inauguration. Or maybe you want to journey from Helena, Montana to the Grand Canyon.

PREPARATION:

- Determine where you will begin the trip and what your final destination will be.

- Calculate the total miles between the two points.

PROCEDURE:

- Have your students run laps around your school track, and convert each lap to one mile of the trip.

- Chart the laps run as miles toward your destination on a class map. For example, if your class is taking a trip from Los Angeles to New York and your students complete 75 laps one day, mark off those 75 miles on a class map. If you would like your kids to make faster progress, you can make each lap equal 10 miles or 100 miles. Kids will run like the wind when they know that their laps count toward a meaningful class project!

VARIATIONS:

- Laps that the kids may do as part of their physical education classes can also count for this project.

- If the distance on your trip is large, choose short-term destinations along the way. Breaking up the trip boosts the feeling of progress and affords you authentic opportunities to study the geography, climate, and culture of these interim locations.

- If you do the calculations as a whole class, your students will have many opportunities to practice their computation skills in an engaging context.

- If you'd rather do this activity without running laps, you can choose another physical activity that involves repetitions, such as jumping jacks, that can later be converted into miles.

Celebrate on the days you arrive at your short-term and long-term destinations!

HEALTH •••••••••••••••••••••••••••••••••••••
SLEEP INTERRUPTION TAG

A variation of the well-known tag game Sharks and Minnows, Sleep Interruption Tag reinforces the importance of getting an uninterrupted night's sleep.

PREPARATION:

- You need a field of a size that works for your students to be able to run across it. The distance from one end line to the other represents the hours of a good night's sleep. (Select the appropriate hours of sleeping. If you ask your students to share their bedtimes, their responses may throw you for a loop!)

- Mark off each hour between the two times with a cone on the side of the field so the kids actually see themselves "running through" each hour of the night.

- Students begin the game by standing on one side of a field ready to run across to the other side.

- A day or two before the game, discuss the causes of sleep interruptions, as well various steps to take to decrease the likelihood that they occur.

PROCEDURE:

- Choose a volunteer to be the first tagger—the dreaded Sleep Interrupter, who represents something that keep us up at night, such as nightmares, thirstiness, loud noises, etc. This first Sleep Interrupter declares his/her specific type of interruption.

- The Sleep Interrupter comes out to the middle of the field, faces everyone else, and prepares to tag as many students as possible as they run across the field.

- The kids represent people who are trying to get a good night's sleep and try to get from one end of the field to the other without being tagged. Everyone tagged by the Sleep Interrupter becomes another Sleep Interrupter during the next round.

- Each new Sleep Interrupter declares aloud the specific type of interruption he/she is pretending to be.

- Play continues until only one sleeper remains, who then gets to celebrate the win by taking a pretend nap as classmates gather around and sing a brief lullaby.

HEALTH ●●●●●●●●●●●●●●●●●●●●●●●●●●●●●●●●●
STRESS TAG

Too much stress can be a problem for many students. This game helps everyone think of ways to handle stress.

PREPARATION:

- Start by discussing with your class what causes them stress—traffic, the loss of a pet, trouble at home, problems with a friend, etc. Then talk about ways to relieve stress—reading, listening to music, talking to a friend, taking a walk, deep breathing, etc.

PROCEDURE:

- Choose three or four kids to be the Stress-Causers, who represent different causes of stress.

- Three or four other kids are chosen to be the Stress-Relievers, who represent a wide variety of stress-relieving strategies, such as reading, listening to music, talking with others, and deep breathing. If possible, the Stress-Relievers carry props with them that reinforce the strategies, such as a book to remind kids to read or a cell phone to remind kids to talk about a problem with a friend.

- Taggers stop people in their tracks when they touch them. Anyone tagged by a Stress-Causer must immediately kneel down.

- Anyone stopped by a Stress-Causer can only re-enter the game after a Stress-Reliever has tagged that student.

This game is full of subtle hints and reminders that help us remember that sometimes in life stress can chase you down—and you have to know how to deal with it.

CHAPTER 5

SONGS FOR LEARNING

SONGS

In *Classroom Activators,* author Jerry Evanski writes, "Music can . . . be used to 'entrain' information into the brain." He uses the word "entrain" to mean helping students learn and memorize information by setting academic content to music. One great way to do this is through the use of familiar tunes. Authors Schwed and Melichar-Utter, in their book *Brain-Friendly Study Strategies, Grades 2-8*, refer to these as "piggyback songs." Setting new words to well-known tunes can help teachers take abstract or potentially confusing content that children would otherwise have to memorize by rote and help them learn it more naturally.

Many of the songs in this chapter go a step further by adding hand and/or body motions to the new words. These movements make the songs even easier to learn and provide an extra way to reinforce the concepts. The songs in this chapter help students learn material in English language arts, math, and science. It's easy to find the tunes to these songs on YouTube or iTunes.

🎵 MATH ●●●●●●●●●●●●●●●●●●●●●●●●●●●●●●●●●
NOW YOU'RE A-OK
AKA "THE DIVISION TERMS SONG"
SUNG TO THE TUNE OF "SURFIN' USA" BY THE BEACH BOYS

Learning the names of each part of a mathematical equation doesn't have to be a dull, tedious exercise in rote memorization. Set to the tune of a Beach Boys classic, this song helps students learn the parts of a division equation: the dividend, divisor, and quotient.

The final two lines in the song are designed to build student confidence. It's as if the song tells children, "If you know your division terms, you're A-OK. Everything is going to be fine."

> **COMMON CORE STANDARDS**
>
> **CCSS.Math.Content.3.OA.A.2**
> **CCSS.Math.Content.4.NBT.B.6**

SONG

With a division sentence
You need to know three terms:

Start with the dividend
It's what you share with friends.

Next door's the divisor
It shows the parts or groups.

The quotient has the last say.
Now you're A-OK!

FROM
STEVE'S CLASSROOM

Kids enjoy serving as leaders for these songs. The song leaders stand and form a rainbow behind their classmates seated in front of the room. Everyone can see the lyrics on the board, and it creates a "surround sound" effect.

♫ MATH ●●●●●●●●●●●●●●●●●●●●●●●●●●●●●●●●●●●●●
FACES, EDGES, VERTICES
SUNG TO THE TUNE OF "ROCK-A-BYE BABY"

Show a diagram of a cube or some other three-dimensional figure for reference and identify the geometry terms on the diagram as your class sings.

COMMON CORE STANDARDS
CCSS.Math.Content.2.G.A.1

SONG

There are three cool parts
To all 3D shapes.
Flat sides go first,
We call each a face.

Next comes the edge,
Where two faces meet.
Edges touch at a vertex,
Now we're complete.

FROM
STEVE'S CLASSROOM

As a general rule, it is a good idea to have some kind of visual available to the students as a reference during these songs.

MATH
YOU GET THE EQUAL SIGN
SUNG TO THE TUNE OF "LOVE POTION NO. 9" BY JERRY LEIBER AND MIKE STOLLER

Consider the following multiple choice question:

COMMON CORE STANDARDS

CCSS.Math.Content.1.OA.D.7
CCSS.Math.Content.3.OA.A.4

$$4 + 8 = \underline{\quad} + 3$$
     A) **12**
     B) **5**
     C) **9**

Many students will jump at choice A because seeing $4 + 8$ will make them think the answer has to be 12. The correct answer, of course, is 9, because we must take all parts of the equation into account, not just the first two numbers.

Kids benefit from viewing algebra questions as a scale that needs balancing, where the left side as a whole unit needs to equal the right side as a whole unit.

PROCEDURE:

Draw this visual on the board while the kids sing "You Get the Get Equal Sign":

$$4 + 8 = 9 + 3$$

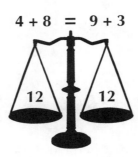

SONG

The left and right sides need to fall in line,
With good balance numbers do align,
And if your answer makes the equation shine,
Then you have shown that—you get the equal sign.

♫ MATH ●●●●●●●●●●●●●●●●●●●●●●●●●●●●●●●●●●●●●●
LINES, RAYS, AND SEGMENTS
SUNG TO THE TUNE OF "SHORTNIN' BREAD"

The hand movements for this song add to the content. A closed fist indicates an endpoint, and a pointed index finger represents "extending forever in one direction."

COMMON CORE STANDARDS

CCSS.Math.Content.4.G.A.1

PROCEDURE:

- Students hold both arms straight out to the side and give the correct combination of fists and pointed fingers as noted for each term in the song.

SONG

Lines, rays, and segments are important,
Lines, rays, and segments are so straight.

A line extends forever in both directions,   *index fingers pointing on both hands*
　　In both directions it's a line.

A ray extends forever in one direction,   *index finger points on one hand; other hand is*
　　In one direction it's a ray.   *a fist*

A segment is something with two endpoints,   *fists on both hands*
　　A segment is a piece of line.

♫ MATH ●●●●●●●●●●●●●●●●●●●●●●●●●●●●●●●●●●●
THE MEASUREMENT CONGA

This song helps to reinforce the relative sizes of measurement units.

There are two ways for your students to move to this song:

> **COMMON CORE STANDARDS**
>
> **CCSS.Math.Content.4.MD.A.1**

1   Safe — students stand behind their chairs, and each does the conga in place.

2   A little trickier to manage, a lot more fun — everyone stands in an actual conga line, moving in a circle around the room. (Try this one with two minutes to go before lunchtime!)

Hand and body movements accompany the song. If the kids form an actual conga line, they will use only body movements since their hands will be on one another's waists. If the kids are behind their desks doing the conga in place, their hands will be free to do the movements.

Any conga tune can be used as the music, but a version of the song that works well for this activity is a conga on iTunes performed by Go, Diego, Go! It takes one minute, 32 seconds—enough for your kids to have a great time!

PROCEDURE:

- While singing the first line, students squat as low as possible to show the smallest of the four measurement units in the song. Students put their hands together to approximate the size of a cup.

- In the next line of the song, they stand a little taller. Students move their hands apart slightly to approximate the size of a pint.

- The kids grow taller once again for the third line of the song (now a quart), and their hands separate a bit more.

- Students sing the last line standing at full height, holding their hands far apart to represent a gallon.

- You can have students sing each line twice before moving on to the next line.

- Repeat the entire song as many times as you can handle!

SONG

Let's start with one cu – up,   *squat low; hands mimic size of a cup*

Two cups make one pi – nt,   *stand a little taller; hands spread apart slightly*

Two pints make one qu – art,   *stand taller; hands spread apart even more*

Four quarts make a gal–lon!   *stand at full height; hands held wide apart*

FROM
STEVE'S CLASSROOM

As a more peaceful alternative to doing the conga, you can help children learn the four measurement units by adapting the Life Cycle of a Butterfly activity from Chapter 4 (page 82). Instead of adjusting the heights of their bodies to show the stages of animal life cycles, the kids begin as cups and attempt to become pints, quarts, and gallons before returning to cups again.

MATH ●●●●●●●●●●●●●●●●●●●●●●●●●●●●●●●●●●●●●
MACARENA MATH

This strategy helps students improve their skip counting while performing the fun and familiar Macarena dance. Thanks to Jeff Haebig for inspiring this activity.

┌─────────────────────────────────────┐
│ **COMMON CORE STANDARDS** │
│ **CCSS.Math.Content.K.CC.A.1** │
│ **CCSS.Math.Content.3.OA.C.7** │
└─────────────────────────────────────┘

PREPARATION:

- Write the multiples vertically on the board or create vertical strips that contain twelve multiples for every number between 3 and 9 (see page 99). Adjust the range for your grade level.

- You need twelve multiples for each number because the Macarena has twelve parts.

- Now you're ready to move!

PROCEDURE:

- Begin with the 5s strip because it is easy to remember. You want everyone to start by learning the song, not trying to keep up with tricky multiples.

- Have the kids stand facing the 5s strip on the board. The music starts, and after the short introductory part of the song, spring into action.

FROM
STEVE'S CLASSROOM

I use iTunes' Sing Pop Radio Hits karaoke version of the Macarena (3:50) for this. We really enjoy doing this song on "Macarena Fridays"!

- For every part of the dance, say a multiple of five. As you turn your right palm down, say *5*. As you turn your left palm down, say *10*. As you turn your right palm up, say *15*. The dance continues until you say the 12th multiple, *60*, as you touch your left hand to your left hip. The Macarena dance calls for participants to shimmy after the twelfth multiple, but there isn't time, because you proceed right to the next number strip.

- When the kids first learn the dance, do two or three strips in a row. Eventually, build up to five or all ten strips.

The length of the karaoke version of the song allows you to proceed through five strips twice or all ten strips once. So, in about four minutes, the kids are seeing, saying, hearing, and moving through these multiples—and having a blast doing it.

MACARENA MATH STRIPS

3	4	5	6	7	8	9
6	8	10	12	14	16	18
9	12	15	18	21	24	27
12	16	20	24	28	32	36
15	20	25	30	35	40	45
18	24	30	36	42	48	54
21	28	35	42	49	56	63
24	32	40	48	56	64	72
27	36	45	54	63	72	81
30	40	50	60	70	80	90
33	44	55	66	77	88	99
36	48	60	72	84	96	108

♫ ENGLISH LANGUAGE ARTS ●●●●●●●●●●●●●●●●●●●●●●
ALL OF US CAN
AKA "THE SIX TRAITS SONG"
SUNG TO THE TUNE OF "THE CANDY MAN" BY LESLIE BRICUSSE AND ANTHONY NEWLEY

This song helps students better understand the key emphases of six important writing traits: Ideas, Conventions, Organization, Word Choice, Sentence Fluency, and Voice.

Many writing programs espouse these traits. One good one is the 6+1 Trait® Writing program. For more information, see educationnorthwest.org/traits.

COMMON CORE STANDARDS

CCSS.ELA-Literacy.W.1.3
CCSS.ELA-Literacy.W.2.3
CCSS.ELA-Literacy.W.3.3
CCSS.ELA-Literacy.W.4.3
CCSS.ELA-Literacy.W.5.3

SONG

Who can do great writing? *(repeat)*
All of us can, *(repeat)*
As long as we remember six important
    traits,
The writing traits, *(repeat)*
The six writing traits. *(repeat)*

Start with Ideas, *(repeat)*
Be sure they make sense, *(repeat)*
Give them a strong focus and enough
    detail,
I – de – as, I – de – as.

Check your Conventions, *(repeat)*
Make everything correct, *(repeat)*
The periods, the commas, the spelling,
    and the caps,
Con – ven – tions, Con – ven – tions.

Now Or – gan – i – za – tion, *(repeat)*
Proceed step–by–step, *(repeat)*
Logical structure and indented para–
    graphs,
Stay or – gan – ized, stay or – gan –
    ized.

Choose your words carefully, *(repeat)*
Have great Word Choice, *(repeat)*
Make them colorful, specific, and strong,
Great Word Choice, great Word Choice.

Sen – tence Flu –en–cy, *(repeat)*
Make every sentence count, *(repeat)*
Try to make e–a–c–h one different from
    the rest,
Craft them well, Craft them well.

Every story needs Voice, *(repeat)*
Your writing sounds like you, *(repeat)*
Your personality should shine right
    through,
There's no one like you, There's no one
    like you.

♪ ENGLISH LANGUAGE ARTS ●●●●●●●●●●●●●●●●●●○○○○
THE BOOK PARTS SONG
SUNG TO THE TUNE OF THE THEME FROM THE '60s TV SHOW, "THE ADDAMS FAMILY"

Elementary students are frequently expected to learn four specific parts of a book: the title page, table of contents, index, and glossary. This song helps make that task an enjoyable event that kids will remember.

> **COMMON CORE STANDARDS**
>
> **CCSS.ELA-Literacy.RI.1.5**
> **CCSS.ELA-Literacy.RI.2.5**
> **CCSS.ELA-Literacy.L.2.4e**

PREPARATION:

- Use sticky notes to make tabs at the beginning of each of these sections to open to each part easily as it comes up in the song. Your students can do the same with their books.

PROCEDURE:

- As the kids are singing the song, hold up a book and display each of these parts.

- Repeat the song twice so the kids receive more practice with these ideas.

SONG

Turn to the front, (snap, snap)
Turn to the front, (snap, snap)
Turn to the front, turn to the front,
    Turn to the front. (snap, snap)

The title page contains
The author and the title
Plus some other info
About how the book was made.

The table of contents
Shows the chapter names
And the page numbers
On which the chapters start.

Turn to the back, (snap, snap)
Turn to the back, (snap, snap)
Turn to the back, turn to the back,
    Turn to the back. (snap, snap)

The glossary is a
Little dictionary
With key words from the book
A-n-d what they mean.

The in-dex shows you
Key terms from the book
And the page numbers
Where they can be found.

ENGLISH LANGUAGE ARTS ●●●●●●●●●●●●●●●●●●●○○○○
THE PREFIX-SUFFIX SONG
SUNG TO THE TUNE OF "IF YOU'RE HAPPY AND YOU KNOW IT"

The hand movements that accompany this song help to reinforce the meaning of the terms *prefix*, *root* or *base word*, and *suffix*.

COMMON CORE STANDARDS

CCSS.ELA-Literacy.RF.2.3d
CCSS.ELA-Literacy.L.2.4b
CCSS.ELA-Literacy.L.2.4c
CCSS.ELA-Literacy.RF.3.3a
CCSS.ELA-Literacy.RF.3.3b
CCSS.ELA-Literacy.L.3.2e

PREPARATION:

Before you begin, write the words *prefix*, *root (or base) word*, and *suffix* on the board as a reference.

- Students start with the their hands low as if they are picking an imaginary "root" word from under the ground and lifting it into position in front of their faces. If you use the term "base word" instead of "root word," tell the kids to pick up an imaginary base from a baseball field and lift it in front of their faces.

- Once the imaginary root or base word is front and center, begin the song.

PROCEDURE:

- On the first line, use your hands to indicate placing the prefix in front of the root or base word. At the end of the line, say *"Pre-fix"* a second time and clap twice as you say it.

- On the second line of the song, use your hands to indicate placing the suffix after the root or base word. At the end of the line, say *"Suf-fix"* a second time and clap twice as you say it.

- Add two claps at the end of the song, for good measure!

SONG

If you add a part to the front, it's a prefix. Pre-fix! (clap, clap on second "Pre-fix")
If you add a part to the end, it's a suffix. Suf-fix! (clap, clap on second "Suf-fix")
If you add a part to the front or add it to the end,
        Now you know it's a prefix or a suffix. (clap, clap)

♪ ENGLISH LANGUAGE ARTS ●●●●●●●●●●●●●●●●●●●●●
NEED TO HAVE A CAP
AKA "THE WHEN TO USE CAPITALS SONG"
SUNG TO THE TUNE OF "OLD MACDONALD"

Nine important capitalization rules are featured in this song. Warning: keeping up the pace with this tune can be a bit tricky! In each stanza, the pace tends to start slowly, speed up through the middle, and slow down again on the last line.

COMMON CORE STANDARDS

CCSS.ELA-Literacy.L.1.2a

CCSS.ELA-Literacy.L.2.2a

CCSS.ELA-Literacy.L.3.2a

CCSS.ELA-Literacy.L.4.2a

SONG

Some words in a sentence need to have
　　caps (need to have a cap).
Days of the week and months of the
　　year need to have a cap.
With a Monday here,
An August there,
Here a day, there a month,
Always caps for days and months,
Some words in a sentence need to have
　　caps (need to have a cap).

The first word of a sentence needs to be
　　capped (needs to have a cap).
With a first word here,
A first word there,
Here a word, there a word,
Always cap the first word,
Some words in a sentence need to have
　　caps (need to have a cap).

Holidays and the word I
　　need to have a cap.
Like Labor Day here,
The word I there,
Holidays, the word I,
Always cap these days and I,
Some words in a sentence need to have
　　caps (need to have a cap).

Events in history and all titles
　　need to have a cap.
Like the Civil War here,
Superfudge there,
History here, a title there,
Forget these rules, you best beware,
Some words in a sentence need to have
　　caps (need to have a cap).

Special events and proper nouns
　　need to have a cap.
With a Book Fair here,
Paris, France there,
Special event, proper noun,
Learn these rules, you'll wear the crown,
Some words in a sentence need to have
　　caps (need to have a cap).

ENGLISH LANGUAGE ARTS
CAUSE AND EFFECT
SUNG TO THE TUNE OF "CAMPTOWN RACES"

Understanding cause and effect is an important reading comprehension skill that children are expected to learn. This song will help your students remember that the cause happens *before* the effect and that the effect cannot happen without the cause.

COMMON CORE STANDARDS

CCSS.ELA-Literacy.RI.3.8
CCSS.ELA-Literacy.RI.4.5
CCSS.ELA-Literacy.RI.5.5
CCSS.ELA-Literacy.L.5.4a

SONG

My untied shoelace made me trip — cause and effect.
The rainstorm made me go inside — cause and effect.
The cause happens first,
The effect happens next.
The effect happens beCAUSE of the cause — cause and effect.

FROM
STEVE'S CLASSROOM

My student volunteers are singing the song in this video: www.youtube.com/watch?v=0Tdr5ylzmG8

SCIENCE
LUNAR CYCLE
SUNG TO THE TUNE OF "FRERE JACQUES"

Hand motions accompany the lyrics of this song to help reinforce the stages of the lunar cycle.

PROCEDURE:

- When singing the lyrics that name a specific lunar cycle phase, make the shape showing the part of the moon that is visible during that phase, as indicated.

- As the class sings the song, display a picture of the lunar cycle phases for reference.

SONG

Lunar cycle
Lunar cycle
Twenty-nine days
Twenty-nine days
New moon, waxing crescent   *Open one hand from a fist into a crescent shape*
New moon, waxing crescent   *Same as above*
First quarter   *Both hands form the shape of a half-moon*
First quarter   *Same as above*

Waxing gibbous   *Both hands create a shape slightly smaller than a full circle*
Waxing gibbous   *Same as above*
A full moon   *Both hands form a full circle*
A full moon   *Same as above*
Now it's getting lighter
Now it's getting lighter
Gra-dual-ly
Gra-dual-ly

Waning gibbous   *Hands move from full circle back to gibbous shape*
Waning gibbous   *Same as above*
Third quarter   *Move from gibbous shape back to half circle*
Third quarter   *Same as above*
Waning crescent, new moon   *Move back to crescent shape and then back to a fist*
Waning crescent, new moon   *Same as above*
Start again
Start again

CHAPTER 6

MOVEMENT BREAKS

MOVEMENT BREAKS

Given the current pressure to address long lists of academic standards in our classrooms, it is tempting for teachers to try to pack as much content as possible into every hour of every day. Time is arguably our most valuable commodity, and it makes sense that we would want to use it efficiently and effectively. But the human brain can only handle so much new learning at once. After working hard on a math activity, for example, children need time to process that new information before moving on to something else. They need time to catch their breath, recharge their batteries, and allow new learning to "settle." Even though the kids may not be aware of it, their brains may still be sorting through the ideas they learned in the last activity as the class launches into a brand new one.

This is why Movement Breaks are so important. Instead of rushing from one learning activity to the next, take a short break (usually one to two minutes) to give students the processing time they need and allow them to downshift. Movement Breaks reenergize the class, increase the sense of connection students feel to one another, and make everyone more cheerful. Movement Breaks require almost no planning, and a repertoire of just four or five ideas will go a long way.

In *The Kinesthetic Classroom*, authors Traci Lengel and Mike Kuczala talk about "brain breaks." They say, "The objective of a brain break is to give the brain time away from the academic content. As students participate in these activities, they are giving their hippocampus (the part of the brain that is responsible for the conversion of working memory to long-term memory) a much-needed break."

Students will take mental breaks throughout the day, whether teachers realize it or not, and those breaks may come at inopportune times. When you schedule breaks into the day and make them novel and interesting, you have much greater control over when the breaks occur and how long they last. Scheduling Movement Breaks helps create a brain-friendly classroom environment that keeps student focus strong throughout the day.

Movement Breaks also give the teacher a moment of set-up time for the next activity, since the kids are usually self-sufficient. The kids are moving while you are prepping. That's a win-win for everyone. If there is nothing you need to prepare, then join right in. (Teachers need breaks, too.)

There are three kinds of Movement Break ideas: 1) individual movements that kids perform alone standing behind their chairs or spread out in open space, 2) partner activities that students do with a neighbor, and 3) movements that involve objects. It requires a bit more time to pass out and collect the objects, but these activities can be especially valuable where classroom teachers are responsible for providing physical education instruction. Small bits of physical education instruction can be incorporated into these Movement Breaks, and they add up throughout the day.

Introduce a new item from this chapter every time your kids need a Movement Break. Over time, you and your students will develop your favorites, and perhaps create your own.

You may find yourself using Movement Breaks more often than you expected. Some experts say that kids should be up and moving every eight minutes; others suggest every ten or twenty. As you get to know your students well, you will develop a good feel for how long they can attend before they need a brief Movement Break.

FROM
STEVE'S CLASSROOM

To expand your collection of Movement Breaks, check out The JAMmin' Minute program (www.jamschoolprogram.com), which offers teachers free, weekly movement routines.

INDIVIDUAL MOVING TO THE MUSIC

This is the most basic Movement Break of them all. Simply put on a song and let the kids move.

If your class seems a bit low energy, consider an upbeat song. If they are overly excited, play a mellow one. Use music to help create the type of environment you want.

As the song plays, students may select from among the five movement choices described in the Morning Warm-Up in Chapter 1 (page 6), or they may just want to follow the beat of the music in a way that seems natural.

As long as the students are keeping their hands to themselves and not bothering their neighbors, the choice of how to move belongs to them. They can dance, stretch, jog in place, or do nothing at all.

FROM STEVE'S CLASSROOM

If I know I'm going to be using a "piggyback" song soon (Chapter 5), I will play that tune during this type of Movement Break. This gives me an opportunity to introduce the song to students who have never heard it before.

FROM STEVE'S CLASSROOM

Some of my favorite songs to get kids moving are "Private Idaho" by the B-52s, "Magic" by B.o.B, "All Star" by Smashmouth, and "Shiny Happy People" by R.E.M. Choose songs that *you* enjoy—movement breaks should be fun for the teacher, too!

INDIVIDUAL ●●●●●●●●●●●●●●●●●●●●●●●●●●●●●●●●
DA DOO RUN RUN

This Movement Break incorporates research about the positive effects on the brain of spinning and body rotation. Authors Lengel and Kuczala recommend spinning movements in their book *The Kinesthetic Classroom*: "Various spinning, balancing, jumping, rolling, turning, and combination activities can help develop and improve the vestibular system and spatial awareness."

PROCEDURE:

- Play the '60s song, "Da Doo Ron Ron," by Jeff Barry, Ellie Greenwich, and Phil Spector.

- During the verses, the students spin slowly.

- When the chorus is sung ("Da Doo Ron Ron Ron, Da Doo Ron Ron"), the kids jog in place. Change the *Rons* to *Runs*.

- The children alternate between slow spinning and quick jogging throughout the song.

INDIVIDUAL ●●●●●●●●●●●●●●●●●●●●●●●●●●●●●●●●
CRISS-CROSS

The midline is the vertical line that divides our body into its left and right halves from head to toe. Crossing this midline with any part of our body builds connections in the brain.

PROCEDURE:

- Begin Criss-Cross by introducing the concept of the midline to your kids. Explain that the brain builds new connections when people cross the midline of their bodies.

- Have them pretend to draw a midline down the middle of their bodies, starting from the top of their heads and proceeding down to their feet.

- Challenge your students to cross the midline as many different ways as they can (i.e., right elbow to left hip, left hand to right ear).

- If you wish, time your students to see how many different ways they can cross the midline in 20 to 30 seconds.

INDIVIDUAL ●●●●●●●●●●●●●●●●●●●●●●●●●●●●●●●●●
STAND OR SIT

This activity develops listening skills, offers a good leg workout, and gives you a chance to bring in a wide variety of topics.

PROCEDURE:

- Standing in front of their chairs, students respond to statements from the teacher by either standing or sitting. For example, say, "Stand if you prefer summer sports; sit if you prefer winter sports."

- In 30 seconds, you can run through four or five of these statements.

VARIATIONS:

- Even though the goal of a Movement Break is not to focus on academic content, you can use Stand or Sit throughout the day to review content quickly and assess understanding. For example, if students are learning the difference between a sentence and a fragment, have them stand in front of their chairs for some quick review. Read various phrases aloud and ask them to stand when they hear complete sentences and sit when they hear fragments. (The subtle message, of course, is that we can't stand for fragments in our own writing.)

- Other examples of using the Stand or Sit method to review:

  - Stand on the healthy food choices; sit on the unhealthy ones

  - Stand on the division word problems that involve sharing; sit on those involving grouping

  - Stand on the subject of the sentence; sit on the predicate

INDIVIDUAL ●●●●●●●●●●●●●●●●●●●●●●●●●●●●●●●● AIR WRITING

Air Writing helps students focus on how to form letters correctly. It works when you are teaching either printing or cursive writing.

PROCEDURE:

- Students imagine a lined piece of paper in front of their faces and "practice" their best printing or cursive writing on that paper. Encourage students to "write" slowly and focus on correct letter formation and size.

- Give them time to write their names, the alphabet, or any special word or phrase you want to highlight at the moment.

VARIATION:

- For an added twist, have the kids write in the air using their elbows, knees, or other body parts.

 INDIVIDUAL ●●●●●●●●●●●●●●●●●●●●●●●●●●●●●●●●●
AS IF

This idea was developed by the Activity Promotion Laboratory of East Carolina University. The title appears to convey a bit of sarcasm, but the actual activity is nothing like that.

PROCEDURE:

- Students act out the following sentences as you read them aloud:
    - "Jog in place **as if** a big scary bear is chasing you."
    - "Walk forwards **as if** you're walking through chocolate pudding."
    - "Jump in place **as if** you're popcorn popping."
    - "Reach up **as if** you're grabbing balloons out of the air."
    - "March in place and play the drums **as if** you are in a marching band."
    - "Paint **as if** the paint brush is attached to your head."
    - "Swim **as if** you are in a giant pool of Jell-O."
    - "Move your feet on the floor **as if** you are ice skating."
    - "Shake your body **as if** you are a wet dog."

VARIATION:

- Have students create and then share some of their own "as ifs."

INDIVIDUAL
TONY CHESTNUT
SUNG BY THE LEARNING STATION

Fun for kids of any age.

PROCEDURE:

- Just start the song "Tony Chestnut," by The Learning Station, and have everyone respond to the lyrics by touching the body parts mentioned. (FYI: the "nut" is the head.)

Be on the lookout for other songs where your kids can move to the lyrics. Some songs will contain lyrics that are fairly literal while others will be more open to interpretation and present tremendous opportunities for student creativity.

FROM
STEVE'S CLASSROOM

Check the YouTube video of The Learning Station folks performing "Tony Chestnut": http://www.youtube.com/watch?v=gESxPhIJbX0.

INDIVIDUAL ●●●●●●●●●●●●●●●●●●●●●●●●●●●●●●●
BEACH PARTY

You can have a one-minute Beach Party any time for a quick break!

PROCEDURE:

- Play any Beach Boys song.

- Have your students move to the song by simulating the activities that people commonly do at the beach—swim, play volleyball, build a sand castle, surf, apply sunscreen, etc.

- Students can stick to one movement through the whole song or change movements as they wish.

INDIVIDUAL SPORTS CENTER

Songs with strong associations to certain sports work well as background theme music to Movement Breaks:

- The theme from *Rocky* ("Gonna Fly Now" by Bill Conti, Carol Connors, and Ayn Robbins): Students pretend to box, do push-ups, run through the streets of Philadelphia, and eat glasses of raw eggs for breakfast.

- The Harlem Globetrotters theme ("Sweet Georgia Brown" by Ben Bernie, Maceo Pinkard, and Kenneth Casey): Kids perform various basketball skills, such as shooting, dribbling, passing, and fancy ball handling.

- "Centerfield" by John Fogerty: Baseball season doesn't officially start each spring until this classic shows up on the radio. Kids run, throw, catch, and swing for the fences.

- "Chariots of Fire" by Vangelis: Students jog in place to the theme from the classic film of the same name.

- The theme music of the Olympics ("Bugler's Dream" by Leo Arnaud): This song can apply to all the events in the Olympic Games and gives kids numerous movement choices to act out.

INDIVIDUAL ●●●●●●●●●●●●●●●●●●●●●●●●●●●●●●
LINE DANCE

Line dances tend to adhere to the familiar structure of four or eight counts of one movement followed by four or eight counts of another, and so on. You can find many videos demonstrating these kid-friendly dances on YouTube.

PROCEDURE:

- Try a simple four- or eight-count line dance with your students.

- If you enjoy this activity and feel ambitious, consider adding more.

VARIATION:

- If you and your students take three to five Movement Breaks on any given day, you can add a different section of a longer line dance during each break. At the end of the day, you can put all the parts of the dance together and perform it before the final bell. This building process from the morning to the afternoon adds great interest and excitement to your day. Performing the dance together will give your class a feeling of accomplishment, improve self-esteem, and increase team bonding. Though it will require instructional time to learn the dance at first, you and your students will be able to perform it from then on and perhaps expand on it or learn new dances in the future.

INDIVIDUAL
THE DEEP FREEZE

Remember the Freeze Dance we learned as kids? You can take that same concept and turn it into an engaging movement break.

PROCEDURE:

- The children stand behind their chairs or in open space.

- Play some up-tempo music. Everyone begins dancing and moving.

- Now turn off the music. The kids freeze and hold their positions as if caught in a giant iceberg.

- After being "frozen" for a few seconds, start the music again.

Every student participates in every round; this is *not* an elimination game.

INDIVIDUAL ●●●●●●●●●●●●●●●●●●●●●●●●●●●●●●●●●●●●
WARM IT UP

This is an especially good idea if your classroom is chilly!

PROCEDURE:

- Students rub their hands together vigorously to generate heat.

- Then they apply their hands to various parts of their faces and bodies to achieve a warming effect.

- The kids can also use their warm hands to give themselves a brief shoulder, neck, back, and arm massage. Very soothing!

INDIVIDUAL
CLAP HANDS

This familiar activity is a guaranteed crowd-pleaser.

PROCEDURE:

- As the teacher or student-leader creates a clapping pattern, the rest of the class responds by matching the sequence, pace, and volume of the pattern.

- Start with a simple pattern and then gradually increase the complexity as students get more comfortable with this activity.

INDIVIDUAL ●●●●●●●●●●●●●●●●●●●●●●●●●●●●●●●●●●●●
TAKE MY BREATH AWAY

Deep breathing is great for a Movement Break when students appear stressed, anxious, or in need of something calming and relaxing. Use any of the breathing variations described in Chapter 1 (page 9).

PROCEDURE:

- Choose one breathing method and have the kids close their eyes and practice it for one minute.

- The goal is for the kids to become internally focused during that minute and increase the duration of their inhales and exhales.

INDIVIDUAL ●●●●●●●●●●●●●●●●●●●●●●●●●●●●●●●●●●●
60-SECOND MENTAL VACATION

There isn't any physical movement in this Movement Break. Only the children's imaginations will be active.

PROCEDURE:

- Ask your kids to stand tall and choose anyplace in the world where they would like to go.

- Encourage them to picture themselves in that place and to see it in as much detail as possible.

- Stop talking and allow them time to drift away and enjoy themselves.

- Gently guide them back to class a minute later, relaxed and refreshed.

INDIVIDUAL ●●●●●●●●●●●●●●●●●●●●●●●●●●●●●●●●●●
STRETCH AND BALANCE

Stretching is a great way to relieve stress.

PROCEDURE:

- You or a student-leader can lead a whole-class stretching session, or the kids can stretch in any way they wish.

- Balancing on one leg or on the toes is a nice challenge to mix into a stretching session.

INDIVIDUAL ●●●●●●●●●●●●●●●●●●●●●●●●●●●●●●
BE POSITIVE

Use this activity to build your students up through positive self-talk and affirmation.

PROCEDURE:

- With the students standing behind their chairs in the "hook-ups" position (page 10), ask them to focus on their strengths or think of times when they accomplished a task successfully, felt the proudest, felt the most determined, or generally felt that they were being their "best selves."

- Students can also tell themselves positive phrases that you suggest or that they create on their own.

INDIVIDUAL ●●●●●●●●●●●●●●●●●●●●●●●●●●●●●●●●●
TENSE AND RELAX

When students feel stress, this activity really helps to relieve it.

PROCEDURE:

- With the children either standing, sitting, or lying on their backs (if you have the space), have them close their eyes and focus on your voice.

- Soft music playing in the background adds a nice calming effect.

- Ask students to tense the muscles in their hands and form a tight fist.

- After 5 to 10 seconds, have them relax their hands completely. Starting with the hands is a great way to introduce the activity because children can control these muscles easily.

- Then, proceeding head to toe, go body part by body part and ask students to clench and then relax those parts in turn.

- Include the muscles in the jaw, arms, back, neck, shoulders, stomach, legs, and feet.

- To conclude the activity, have the students tense all their muscles at once and then relax them.

We all carry tension in different places in our bodies and it is important to identify these spots and learn to relax them.

PARTNERS ●●●●●●●●●●●●●●●●●●●●●●●●●●●●●
MIRRORING

Mirroring is a enjoyable activity that students do in pairs.

PROCEDURE:

- Pair students in any way that works for you.

- In pairs, students face each other with one partner serving as leader.

- The leader creates various hand, arm, and body movements.

- The follower tries to match the leader as precisely as possible—same movements, same speed.

- The leader and follower switch roles halfway through.

- Challenge the pairs to reach the point where they become so proficient, observers have difficulty determining who is leading and who is following.

VARIATIONS:

- Try "One-Behinds." When the leader begins the second movement, the follower begins the first movement. When the leader moves to the third movement, the follower begins the second—always one behind. You can easily turn Mirroring and One-Behinds into whole-class activities, where one person (teacher or student) acts as the leader, and the whole class either mirrors the movements or follows one move behind.

- To add music to the Mirroring activity, play Michael Jackson's "Man in the Mirror" as the kids are moving. (Thanks to physical education teacher Seth Martin for that suggestion.)

PARTNERS
SECRET HANDSHAKES

Children really enjoy these creative handshakes.

PROCEDURE:

- Lumberjack: Students extend their hands out straight with their thumbs up. The kids grab each other's thumbs with their open hands to create one connected "saw." Once the saw has been formed, the children make long, slow strokes back and forth to cut the wood.

- Salmon: Students gently slap their flat, open right hands together.

- Milking the Cow: One student serves as the cow and makes two fists with thumbs pointing down. The other squeezes the two thumbs to simulate milking the cow.

VARIATION:

- After you have introduced these handshakes, ask each pair to create its own three-part handshake. The pairs can include any hand movements that they want to string together. Over time you can build up to five or even ten-part handshakes. This is a great way to strengthen students' memories, improve cooperation, and increase team bonding.

PARTNERS
WALK 'N' TALK

This activity allows students to pair up and discuss any subject. It is especially useful when students have been working quietly for a while and need a chance to talk.

PROCEDURE:

- Pair students in any way that works for you.

- The students walk in pairs around a track or around the room. They talk about a variety of academic and non-academic topics that you pose, such as their favorite subjects, favorite movies, favorite sports, or favorite games.

- Every time the children start a new lap, present a new topic. For example, as the whole group prepares to begin its first lap, you can call out, "Discuss your favorite movie and why it's your favorite." Before the second lap, announce, "Discuss your favorite sport and why it's your favorite."

VARIATIONS:

- You can use the Walk 'n' Talk at the end of lessons to offer students an active way to reflect and further cement the learning. Choose an academic topic that relates to an activity you have recently concluded. For example, if you have finished a math activity in which the kids chose strategies to solve open-ended problems, you can have kids talk about which strategy they felt was most effective and why.

- The Walk 'n' Talk can also be used during instructional lessons as an effective variation of the traditional "think-pair-share" strategy in which students have time to think privately about an idea, turn and talk to a partner about it, and then participate in a whole-class share. During the "pair" part, instead of having the kids turn and talk with a neighbor, you can ask them to walk and talk with a neighbor.

FROM
STEVE'S CLASSROOM

I've found that shy or quiet children are sometimes more likely to participate in pair conversations during a Walk 'n' Talk, rather than when everyone is seated in close proximity to one another.

PARTNERS ●●●●●●●●●●●●●●●●●●●●●●●●●●●●●●●●
TASK CHALLENGES

Posing specific task challenges offers novelty and builds cooperation within your class.

PROCEDURE:

- Give your students a brief task challenge sheet that they must complete in pairs (see page 133 for a Partner Challenges sheet you can use or adapt). The list of challenges should include a variety of physical challenges, such as performing 10 jumping jacks and balancing on one leg for 15 seconds. You can also build in novel items, such as creating a new three-part handshake, walking one lap around the room to talk about your favorite book, or giving two compliments to your partner.

- Students can proceed through the entire list in one Movement Break, or you can spread the tasks over a period of days.

VARIATION:

- You can modify the Partner Challenges sheet for your age group.

Name: _____ Date: _____

PARTNER CHALLENGES

_____ **1** I did 15 jumping jacks with my partner.

_____ **2** My partner and I each balanced on one leg for 15 seconds.

_____ **3** Then we each balanced on the other leg for 15 seconds.

_____ **4** My partner and I walked one lap around the room to discuss our favorite books.

_____ **5** I flipped an imaginary pancake with my partner seven times.

_____ **6** My partner and I created a new three-part handshake.

_____ **7** My partner and I hopped on each leg 10 times.

_____ **8** I jogged in place for 30 seconds with my partner.

_____ **9** My partner and I created a new five-part "patty cake" routine.

_____ **10** My partner and I gave each other two compliments about something important, such as our character traits, work habits, or social skills.

Bonus: Do this next activity only after you and your partner have finished all the other activities.

_____ My partner and I invented our own activity using classroom supplies or a piece of playground equipment.

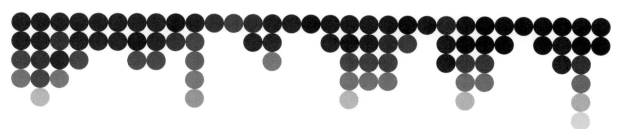

OBJECTS ●●●●●●●●●●●●●●●●●●●●●●●●●●●●●●●●●●●
BEAN BAGS

In this activity, students attempt various bean bag challenges to develop hand-eye coordination, motor skills, and proficiency with both hands. You can easily stretch the activities out from a two-minute Movement Break to a 20-minute physical education lesson, especially on rainy days.

PROCEDURE:

Ask your kids, "Can you...

- Do a figure eight through your legs with your bean bag?

- Pass the bean bag around your waist quickly clockwise? Counter-clockwise?

- Put the bean bag on your head, drop it forward, and catch it before it hits the ground? How about dropping it backward?

- Toss the bean bag in the air and catch it before it hits the ground? Clap once before it hits the ground? Twice? How many claps can you do?"

- Toss the bean bag with your left hand in a rainbow shape and catch it with your right hand? The other way?" (Students who have trouble with this task may have visual tracking issues and struggle with reading fluency. Observe your kids closely as they perform this task to determine whether any follow-up is needed.)

FROM
STEVE'S CLASSROOM

Make these challenges open-ended so that kids who are able to move to higher levels of difficulty have the opportunity. This is effective differentiated instruction.

OBJECTS
CUPSTACKING

The sport of Cupstacking has become increasingly popular in recent years. It calls for individuals to arrange a set of cups into various pyramid-shaped formations as quickly as possible. Stacking cups improves students' ability to use both hands, cross the midline, and focus. If you have a class set of cups at your school, you may want to try

FROM
STEVE'S CLASSROOM

For more information about Cupstacking, visit speedstacks.com.

introducing Cupstacking to your students as a new Movement Break. The cups can be used in many different ways and can be incorporated into a wide variety of fitness activities.

PROCEDURE:

- Students can take out their individual set of 12 cups and practice arranging the 3, the 6, and the 10, or proceed through the entire cycle.

⊛ OBJECTS ●●●●●●●●●●●●●●●●●●●●●●●●●●●●●●●●●●●
COUNT YOUR STEPS

Pedometers (step counters) are great resources to have in the classroom, but ones that work reliably are relatively expensive. Many people report that when they wear pedometers they are more aware of their daily activity levels and make greater efforts to move around all day.

PROCEDURE:

- If you have access to pedometers for each student, have them wear them. Students clip these devices to their waists and use them to count the number of steps they take each day.

- During Movement Breaks, give everyone a chance to move around the room and increase their step totals. Some kids will walk around with a friend, others will jog in place, and, of course, some children will run in place as if they are in the Olympics!

- Graph the results at the end of each day so students can assess their progress and have authentic experience incorporating math skills into their daily lives.

CHAPTER 7

RHYTHMS AND CHANTS

RHYTHMS AND CHANTS

This chapter includes a variety of teaching strategies consistent with the Total Physical Response (TPR) approach developed by James Asher that aids students in their understanding of academic concepts through the use of hand and body movements. You can use these ideas to introduce new content, reinforce and practice familiar concepts, and assess student proficiency. If an activity in this chapter is presented for one purpose (e.g., assessing student proficiency), and you'd like to use it for a different purpose (e.g., introducing new content), simply alter the amount of support you provide and adjust the pace to achieve your desired outcome.

The rhythms and chants are short and simple. They can be incorporated into your instructional practice easily without much preparation. Repeating the words and corresponding movements helps kids learn important information and transfer it to long-term memory. Employing these ideas for one minute a day over a period of days can produce impressive results. After you do the rhythms and chants with your students, you can reinforce these ideas by using them as future Movement Breaks, since the kids will already be familiar with the content.

FROM
STEVE'S
CLASSROOM

If I use an activity to introduce new material, I will proceed slowly, provide cues, and model the appropriate actions. When I use the same activity for assessment purposes, I quicken the pace and don't provide any support because I want to see what my students know.

ENGLISH LANGUAGE ARTS ●●●●●●●●●●●●●●●●●●●●
SUBJECT AND PREDICATE

This chant, along with its corresponding hand motions, helps students learn the two parts of a sentence.

COMMON CORE STANDARDS

CCSS.ELA-Literacy.L.3.1i
CCSS.ELA-Literacy.L.4.1f

CHANT	DIRECTIONS
Sub - ject,	*Clap hands on each syllable*
Who or what the sentence is about.	*Turn your palms up and sway from side to side, as if asking a question*
Pre - di - cate,	*Clap hands on each syllable*
What happens.	*Lift your voice on the word "happens."*

Repeat the entire chant two or three times.

ENGLISH LANGUAGE ARTS ●●●●●●●●●●●●●●●●●●●●●●●●●
MAKING AN INFERENCE

One of the most important comprehension skills that students learn in elementary school is how to make an inference. When students don't find a specific answer in the text, they look for a clue in the text that must be combined with their own knowledge to produce an inference.

In this chant, the kids repeat the words to this "equation" while performing the hand motions:

> **COMMON CORE STANDARDS**
>
> **CCSS.ELA-Literacy.RL.4.1**
> **CCSS.ELA-Literacy.RI.4.1**

STORY CLUE   +   MY OWN KNOWLEDGE   =   INFERENCE

Do this chant in "call and response" format every day when the students are learning about making inferences.

YOU SAY	THE KIDS SAY
"Story Clue"	**"Story Clue"** *Put palms together and then open the hands as if opening a book*
"Plus"	**"Plus"** *Make the addition sign with the forearms*
"My own knowledge"	**"My own knowledge"** *Point to the brain*
"Equals"	**"Equals"** *Make equal sign with forearms*
"Inference"	**"Inference"** *Make capital "I" with hands: one hand vertical, the other hand going back and forth to make the top and bottom horizontal lines*

ENGLISH LANGUAGE ARTS
ALLITERATIONS

In *Classroom Activators,* Jerry Evanski describes an activity called "Motion Potion," and recommends it "as an excellent tool for learning and remembering names at the start of a course." This kind of chant gives students practice in creating alliteration.

COMMON CORE STANDARDS
CCSS.ELA-Literacy.RL.2.4

PROCEDURE:

- The whole class stands in a circle.

- Each student takes a turn forming an alliteration by combining his/her first name with an adjective that describes the student and begins with the same letter as the student's name. For example: *Sensitive Sarah, Responsible Robert, Jolly Jessie.*

- Each student says his/her alliteration and creates a hand or body movement that matches it.

- After each student's turn, the whole class repeats the alliteration and performs the movement.

ENGLISH LANGUAGE ARTS
CURSIVE WRITING

Use this chant if your students practice cursive writing on paper with three lines (solid top and bottom lines and a dotted middle line). It helps raise their awareness of proper letter height.

PROCEDURE:

- Call out a letter.
- The following body parts correspond to various parts of the lined paper:
  - **Top of Head:** Upper solid line
  - **Shoulders:** Dotted middle line
  - **Waist:** Solid bottom line
  - **Feet:** The solid line below the bottom solid line.

Example: call out "lower case *h*."

First, students touch the body part that corresponds to the *lowest* line the letter *h* touches (waist).

Second, students touch the body part corresponding to the *highest* line the letter *h* touches (top of head).

ENGLISH LANGUAGE ARTS
CSI

This chant helps children understand the difference between proper and common nouns. The chant itself emphasizes the two factors that distinguish a proper noun from a common noun:

<table>
<tr><td colspan="2">COMMON CORE STANDARDS</td></tr>
</table>

COMMON CORE STANDARDS

CCSS.ELA-Literacy.L.1.2a
CCSS.ELA-Literacy.L.2.2a
CCSS.ELA-Literacy.L.3.2a
CCSS.ELA-Literacy.L.4.2a

1   Proper nouns are capitalized

2   Proper nouns name specific people, places, and things

PROCEDURE:

- Write this on the board and refer to it when performing the "call and response" chant:

    C - capital letter

    S - specific person, place, or thing

    I - I know the difference

YOU SAY	THE KIDS SAY
"C"	*"C"*
"Capital letter"	**"Capital letter"** *as they put their hands high in the air, showing the height of a capital letter*
"S"	*"S"*
"Specific person, place, or thing"	**"Specific person, place, or thing"** *as everyone points to one proper noun in the room*
"I"	*"I"*
"I know the difference"	**"I know the difference"** *as they point both thumbs to themselves*

ENGLISH LANGUAGE ARTS
THE FIVE Ws CHANT

This simple "call and response" chant helps students remember the five Ws that are so important for clear writing.

YOU SAY	THE KIDS SAY
"Who"	"Who" *and point to self*
"What"	"What" *and shrug their shoulders*
"Where"	"Where" *and look around with one hand over eyebrows*
"When"	"When" *and look at the wrist (as if looking at a watch)*
"Why"	"Why" *and form "Y" with arms and body*

ENGLISH LANGUAGE ARTS ●●●●●●●●●●●●●●●●●●●●●●●●●
FOUR TYPES OF SENTENCES

This is a whole-class activity that includes a chant plus movement. It helps students learn the four types of sentences.

COMMON CORE STANDARDS

CCSS.ELA-Literacy.L.1.1j

PREPARATION:

- Each student needs a dry-erase board and a marker.

PROCEDURE:

- The students write one fact about themselves on their dry-erase boards in the form of a statement. The kids usually have no trouble with this initial step because we typically share information through statements.

FROM
STEVE'S CLASSROOM

Any time we personalize an activity, engagement and motivation automatically increase.

- Each student writes a second fact about themselves, but this time the information must be phrased as a question. Examples: "Do you know I like to read?" and "Can we eat some broccoli now because I love dark green vegetables?"

- The students write a third fact using commands. This is usually the most challenging part of the activity. Counter the notion of having to be forceful by encouraging everyone to initiate their commands with the word *please* and use a soft tone of voice when sharing their ideas aloud. Examples: "Please take me to the comic book store because I love reading comics." and "Please bring me some grapes because they are my favorite fruit."

- Students create exclamatory sentences to share information about themselves. Examples: "I love reading!" and "Don't make me leave here at 3:00 p.m. because I don't want to stop learning!"

- As you proceed through the activity, incorporate four movements for the four types of sentences, using a call-and-response chant.

YOU SAY	THE KIDS SAY
"Statement"	**"Statement"** *Students slump their shoulders and use a plain, "ho-hum" voice (since statements are usually said in a calm, ordinary manner)*
"Question" *Lift your voice as you say the word*	**"Question"** *Students shrug their shoulders and lift their arms as if asking something*
"Command"	**"Command"** *Students point straight ahead*
"Exclamation"	**"Exclamation"** *Students say the word with strong emotion while forming an exclamation point with their arms (one forearm held vertically, and the other fist held below the forearm to serve as the dot of the exclamation point)*

MATH
ROUNDING CHANT

This chant, along with its corresponding hand motions, helps students grasp the concept of rounding to the nearest ten. It reminds them to look at the number in the ones place for guidance.

If the digit in the ones
Is zero through four,
Keep the tens digit on the floor.
If the digit in the ones
Is five or above,
Take the tens digit and give it a shove.

"Keep the tens digit on the floor" means to keep the number the same, while "give a shove" means to increase by one.

Before beginning the chant, have your students place their hands in front of them, palms up, with their left hands representing the tens place and their right hands the ones.

Hand motions that go along with the chant:

CHANT	DIRECTIONS
"If the digit in the ones"	*point to the right palm with the left index finger (this move helps ensure that students know which place is which)*
"Is zero through four"	*make the shape of a zero with the fingers of one hand, then a hyphen on "through," then hold up four fingers*
"Keep the tens digit on the floor."	*point downward at the flat, open left palm with the right index finger (as if keeping the tens digit down)*
"If the digit in the ones"	*point again to their right palms with the left index finger*
"Is five or above"	*hold up five fingers on one hand and then point straight up*

"Take the tens digit and give it a shove." | point to the left palm with the right index finger and then turn the right index finger up to represent "giving that digit a shove." Use only one pointer finger to represent increasing the tens digit by one.

MATH ●●●●●●●●●●●●●●●●●●●●●●●●●●●●●●●●●
THREE KINDS OF ANGLES

Jean Blaydes of Action Based Learning inspired this idea that helps kids distinguish among three types of angles: acute, right, and obtuse.

- For right angles: students spread their thumbs as far away from their index fingers as possible to make a square corner. As the kids display their hands this way, they say, "Right on!"

- For acute angles (less than 90 degrees): students hold their index fingers and thumbs close together (as if they are looking at some precious, tiny little creature) and say, "Ah, cute" (because little things are often cute).

- For obtuse angles (greater than 90 degrees): students make a fist and extend their pinky fingers and thumbs out to the sides. The thumbs and pinkies form an obtuse angle. The children shake their hands back and forth and say, "Hang loose, obtuse."

FROM
STEVE'S
CLASSROOM

My student volunteers demonstrate these hand motions in this video: www.youtube.com/watch?v=5kt9i7rlrBM

SCIENCE ●●●●●●●●●●●●●●●●●●●●●●●●●●●●●●●●●●●
THE HUMAN THERMOMETER

This chant, along with its corresponding hand motions, helps students learn the relationship between the Fahrenheit and Celsius temperature scales.

PROCEDURE:

- Standing tall, the students use their bodies to represent a thermometer. One side of the body represents the Fahrenheit scale; the other, the Celsius scale. This "call and response" activity includes both of these scales.

- Start with only one scale and introduce each scale separately. Use the odd-numbered steps for Fahrenheit, and the even-numbered steps for Celsius. Combine them when your class is ready.

- The feet represent the freezing point of each scale, and the head, the boiling point. The knees, waist, and shoulders correspond to specific points on the thermometer.

- The students stand facing the teacher. Proceed with the following call-and-response statements, with the students repeating everything you say and do.

- Post a picture of a thermometer at the front of the room as a reference point to assist students throughout this activity.

1 Sweep your right hand down the right side of your body from head to toe and say "Fahrenheit."

2 Sweep your left hand down the left side of your body from head to toe and say "Celsius."

3 Touch your right foot, say, "32 degrees Fahrenheit," shiver, and say, "Brrr, freezing!"

4 Touch your left foot, say, "0 degrees Celsius," shiver, and say, "Brrr, freezing!"

5 Touch your right knee, say, "75 degrees Fahrenheit," relax, and say, "Ahh, warm."

6 Touch your left knee, say, "25 degrees Celsius," relax, and say, "Ahh, warm."

7 Touch your right waist, say, "120 degrees Fahrenheit," lift your feet as if walking through hot sand, and say, "Hot, hot!"

8 Touch your left waist, say, "50 degrees Celsius," lift your feet as if walking through hot sand, and say, "Hot, hot!"

9 Touch your right shoulder, say, "170 degrees Fahrenheit," lift your feet as if walking on hot coals, and say, "Super hot!"

10 Touch your left shoulder, say, "75 degrees Celsius," lift your feet as if walk-

ing on hot coals, and say, "Super hot!"

11 Touch the right side of your head, say, "212 degrees Fahrenheit," swoon as if about to melt, and say, "Boiling!"

12 Touch the left side of your head, say, "100 degrees Celsius," swoon as if about to melt, and say, "Boiling!"

Though the temperatures on each side of the body do not correlate exactly with the Fahrenheit-Celsius conversion scale (F = 9/5 C + 32), they are close. These back-and-forth, side-by-side comparisons help students develop a better understanding of how the Fahrenheit temperatures connect to the less familiar Celsius scale.

VARIATION:

- Once you have gone through these steps a few times, mix things up and conduct a mini-assessment. For example, say, "Zero degrees Celsius," and the children will touch their feet and say, "Freezing." Next, say, "One hundred degrees Celsius," and the kids will touch their heads and respond, "Boiling!" Continue calling out random locations on the thermometer so there is no predictable pattern for the class to follow. After you have introduced The Human Thermometer to your students, this activity can serve as a Movement Break (Chapter 6). It will provide valuable reinforcement for students who need more practice with these concepts.

SCIENCE ●●●●●●●●●●●●●●●●●●●●●●●●●●●●●●
LAYERS OF THE RAINFOREST

Students touch various body parts to learn the relative locations of the four layers of the rainforest.

PROCEDURE:

- When you're first teaching the rainforest, conduct this activity slowly in call-and-response format, starting at the bottom of the rainforest and proceeding upwards.

YOU SAY	THE KIDS SAY
"Rivers and forest floor"	**"Rivers and forest floor"** *and touch their feet*
"Understory"	**"Understory"** *and touch their waists*
"Canopy"	**"Canopy"** *and touch their shoulders*
"Emergent layer"	**"Emergent layer"** *and touch the top of their heads*

VARIATIONS:

- After the students have learned the layers, use the activity for assessment purposes or as a Movement Break.

- To see who really knows the layers, call out a layer while touching an incorrect body part to see who simply follows what you do and who knows better.

CHAPTER 8

CREATING A QUALITY CLASSROOM CULTURE
WITH MOVEMENT AND STORIES

MOVEMENT AND STORIES

Team-building, cooperation among students, and management of the classroom can all be enhanced with a variety of movement activities and stories.

At the beginning of each school year, it is critical to build a cooperative classroom culture so students feel safe and comfortable and see one another as friends and assets, not rivals.

We know that our students pay close attention to what we say and do at the beginning of the year. When we model the behaviors we want our students to use—using a positive tone of voice, saying *please* and *thank you*, and looking out for the well-being of others—we begin to create a classroom where our students will feel comfortable and thrive.

Icebreaking and team-building activities play an important role in this process. They give kids a chance to get to know one another while giving us a chance to highlight the positive qualities and traits that we want to build into the foundation of our classroom. Icebreaking and team-building movement activities help to establish a positive tone right from the start. Spread out these icebreaking and team-building activities over the first few weeks. Then continue to emphasize the importance of building an upbeat, friendly classroom environment using the brainstorming and sharing activities along with the classroom management ideas.

BONDING AND TEAM BUILDING ●●●●●●●●●●●●●●●●●●
HIGH-FIVING

Students walk through the room "high-fiving" their classmates. Each time the students give a high-five, they look the other person in the eye and tell the other person their name. It's a terrific idea when you have a few spare minutes and want the kids to learn one another's names in an active way.

BONDING AND TEAM BUILDING ●●●●●●●●●●●●●●●●●●
HUMAN HEALTH HUNT

A variation of the People Hunt activity in Jeanne Gibbs' 1987 book *Tribes: A Process for Social Development and Cooperative Learning,* the Human Health Hunt promotes positive social interactions, creates situations where students need to help one another, and raises awareness of important health concepts. Jeff Haebig uses the Human Health Hunt in his workshops.

PREPARATION:

- Duplicate one Human Health Hunt sheet (page 160) for each student.

PROCEDURE:

- The students walk around the room with their Human Health Hunt sheet and collect the signatures of classmates who exemplify one or more of the behaviors described.

- Each student may sign a given paper only once, to ensure that everyone mingles with as many people as possible.

- Each student may also sign his/her own paper once.

- You can end the activity with a whole-class debriefing so that everyone has a chance to share. Go down the page item by item and ask students to raise their hands if they either signed a classmate's paper for that item or could have signed for that item.

Name:_____

HUMAN HEALTH HUNT

1 _____ doesn't add salt to food.

2 _____ exercises regularly to stay in shape.

3 _____ usually eats a healthy breakfast.

4 _____ fastens his/her seat belt in a car.

5 _____ is careful not to eat too much sugar.

6 _____ loves being a student.

7 _____ wears sunscreen to protect his/her skin.

8 _____ will always be a non-smoker.

9 _____ regularly reads for pleasure.

10 _____ likes wheat bread more than white bread.

11 _____ enjoys a good, hard workout.

12 _____ flosses every day.

13 _____ brings healthy snacks to school.

14 _____ tries to avoid fried and fatty foods.

15 _____ has looked forward to the start of school.

16 _____ is an enthusiastic swimmer.

17 _____ has given up an unhealthy habit.

18 _____ doesn't drink too many soft drinks.

19 _____ likes at least two vegetables.

20 _____ tries to think positively at all times.

BONDING AND TEAM BUILDING ●●●●●●●●●●●●●●●●●●●●●
COOPERATIVE HANDSHAKE

According to physical education teacher Melanie Champion, this activity builds listening skills, challenges short-term memory, and improves cooperation.

PREPARATION:

- Think up (and maybe make a list of) handshake movements that students can perform.

- Pair up students any way you choose.

PROCEDURE:

- Partners start on opposite sides of any indoor or outdoor space.

- The teacher calls out the first handshake movement, such as a left-handed fist bump, and the partners walk towards each other and perform the task. They then return to their starting positions. The teacher calls out the second movement, such as "touch right elbows," and the partners again walk toward each other, perform the fist bump and then add the elbow touch.

- Add moves to the sequence until you reach a number that is appropriate for your students.

- Other potential handshake movements include "high tens," "low tens," "toes to toes," and "shoulder to shoulder."

VARIATION:

- Challenge your students to create their own handshake moves and share them with the whole class.

BONDING AND TEAM BUILDING ●●●●●●●●●●●●●●●●●●●
CATCH MY NAME?

Catch My Name? is adapted from the Name Game activity in Brenda Utter's book *Pick and Plan: 100 Brain-Compatible Strategies for Lesson Design*. It helps students learn one another's names quickly when school begins.

PROCEDURE:

- Students stand in a circle and take turns throwing underhand to one another any unlikely-to-cause-an-injury-and-make-someone-cry-on-the-first-day-of-school item, such as a Koosh ball, bean bag, or other type of soft ball.

- Every time a student catches the ball, that student says his/her name aloud.

- Establish an order for the throwing and catching. Proceed through this order once or twice or until students become comfortable with the activity and then speed things up a little.

VARIATIONS:

- Have the throwers say the name of the person to whom they are throwing.

- Consider using multiple balls at once.

BRAINSTORMING AND SHARING ●●●●●●●●●●●●●●●●●●
I'VE GOT AN IDEA!

This idea facilitates idea sharing through social interaction.

PREPARATION:

- Give each student a piece of blank 8-1/2 X 11-inch sheet of paper.

PROCEDURE:

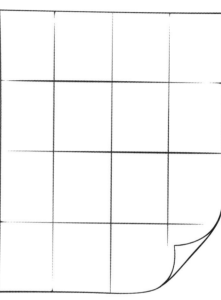

- Have students fold the blank sheet of paper into 16 squares, or whatever number you think is appropriate for the number of ideas you expect your students to brainstorm.

- Announce the topic for brainstorming and ask your students to come up with ideas on the topic.

- Students write one idea in each square.

- Most likely, they will not use all 16 squares right away, but they will fill them in as they share ideas with other students. If they fill all their squares with their own ideas, they can use the back or create more by folding the paper into more squares.

- After a few minutes of independent brainstorming, everyone stands up and finds a partner.

- The kids each give one of their ideas to their partners and get one from their partners.

- Once both partners have recorded their new ideas in open squares, they thank each other and find new partners.

- This interaction continues for a few minutes before the activity concludes with a whole-class share, during which participants can add even more ideas to their papers.

BRAINSTORMING AND SHARING ●●●●●●●●●●●●●●●●●●○○
THE WALKING PAIR SHARE

You can use the "Walk 'n' Talk" strategy described in Chapter 6 (page 131) as a method for students to share ideas that they have just brainstormed.

COMMON CORE STANDARDS
CCSS.ELA-Literacy.SL.2.1

PROCEDURE:

- Have kids walk around the room or an outdoor area and share their brainstormed ideas.

VARIATION:

- Students can walk the entire time with one partner or switch partners along the way to share ideas with several people.

BRAINSTORMING AND SHARING ●●●●●●●●●●●●●●●●● ● ● ●
ROTATION

Rotation works well when you want students to complete a series of short, separate tasks. It's easiest to describe this activity using an example: studying the style of artist Vincent van Gogh.

PREPARATION:

- Place approximately 10-12 reproductions of van Gogh's paintings around the room.

- Pair students in whatever way you choose.

PROCEDURE:

- Working in pairs, the kids spend a few minutes at each station, noting specific observations pertaining to van Gogh's use of line, color, shapes, and other elements.

- Everyone can move in a pre-determined order or at random, as long as no more than one or two groups are stopped at any one station.

VARIATIONS:

- Students can each carry their own note-taking sheets, or you can place papers at each station so that everyone makes their observations about the artwork in the same place. If you have a sheet at each station, each pair can read what the previous pairs wrote and add their own ideas. At the end, you will have a cumulative record of all the contributions made at every station.

- You can also take the opposite approach, with the kids remaining seated and rotating the materials around the room. For example, at the end of each Reading Workshop unit, you can have a "Shopping Day," that give kids the opportunity to look at the two to three dozen book options available for the next unit and rank their top choices on an index card. Rotating the books around the room simplifies the activity.

BRAINSTORMING AND SHARING ●●●●●●●●●●●●●●●●●
GALLERY WALK

Once the kids have completed an art project, a math problem-solving challenge, or any other type of activity where students are demonstrating a wide variety of strategies or unique ways of thinking, consider a Gallery Walk. The Gallery Walk allows every child to see every other child's work.

PREPARATION:

- Students display their work on desks. A horseshoe or circle formation is ideal.

PROCEDURE:

- Everyone walks around the room slowly (keeping their hands to themselves) and looks at the projects on top of each desk.

- Emphasize the importance of walking quietly and paying close attention to everyone's efforts, not just those of their closest friends.

- To heighten students' focus, provide instructions in advance about the specific features of the work to which you want everyone to attend.

- A whole-class debriefing should follow a Gallery Walk. This affords students the opportunity to describe noteworthy examples of quality work that they saw, ask questions, and give compliments. This is also the time for you to follow up about the specific features you asked everyone to notice.

CLASSROOM MANAGEMENT ●●●●●●●●●●●●●●●●●●
PERSONAL STORYTELLING

Imagine that when your students return from music class one day, the music teacher informs you that she observed some of them insulting a child from another class. You know you need to address this situation back in your classroom, but how? Do you scream? Punish? Lecture?

Sometimes the best method is to tell a story. The kids aren't expecting this, and as a result, they will listen carefully and respect the restraint and calmness you demonstrate. Gather the class together and tell a story about a time when you were their age and treated someone the way the music teacher said they just treated somebody. Tell them what happened, how bad you felt inside, how embarrassed you were, how you didn't want to develop that type of reputation, and how you tried later that day to make it up to the person you offended.

Sharing personal stories is perhaps the most powerful move teachers have in their repertoire, and students will take away far more from a story than they will from a tirade or a lecture. Of course, when student misbehavior occurs, we often need to do more than just tell a story, following through with consequences. But telling the right story at the right time can be the most effective step we can take to change behavior.

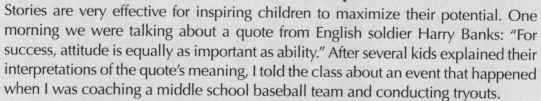

FROM
STEVE'S CLASSROOM

Stories are very effective for inspiring children to maximize their potential. One morning we were talking about a quote from English soldier Harry Banks: "For success, attitude is equally as important as ability." After several kids explained their interpretations of the quote's meaning, I told the class about an event that happened when I was coaching a middle school baseball team and conducting tryouts.

Unfortunately, we could only keep 12 of the 16 kids who were seeking a spot on the squad because our team van could only seat 12 players. During batting practice one day, a ball got away and was rolling down the right field line. The next thing I knew, a boy named Mike began sprinting from his spot all the way over in left field to retrieve the loose ball. Every other player on the field was closer to the ball than Mike, but he chased it down first because he wanted to show me how badly he wanted to be on the team. Mike was not the biggest, fastest, or most skilled player on the team, and based on talent alone, he might not have made the squad. But because of his attitude, his hustle, and his determination, he did make the team, and he went on to become a valuable contributor.

My kids loved hearing this story, and I think they learned an important lesson. Look for opportunities to share your stories with your class to inspire your students.

COMMON CORE STANDARDS ALIGNMENT

KINDERGARTEN

MATH

Counting and Cardinality

CCSS.Math.Content.K.CC.A.1...**Macarena Math** (p. 98)
Count to 100 by ones and by tens.

CCSS.Math.Content.K.CC.A.3...**Jump Ropes for Math** (p. 24)
Write numbers from 0 to 20. Represent a number of objects with a written numeral 0-20 (with 0 representing a count of no objects).

Geometry

CCSS.Math.Content.K.G.A.2...**Jump Ropes for Math** (p. 24)
Correctly name shapes regardless of their orientations or overall size.

CCSS.Math.Content.K.G.B.5...**Jump Ropes for Math** (p. 24)
Model shapes in the world by building shapes from components (e.g., sticks and clay balls) and drawing shapes.

CCSS.Math.Content.K.G.B.6...**Jump Ropes for Math** (p. 24)
Compose simple shapes to form larger shapes.

ENGLISH LANGUAGE ARTS

Language

CCSS.ELA-Literacy.L.K.1d...**The Five Ws Chant** (p. 146)
Understand and use question words (interrogatives) (e.g., who, what, where, when, why, how).

CCSS.ELA-Literacy.L.K.5b...**The Jumping Game** (p. 52)
Demonstrate understanding of frequently occurring verbs and adjectives by relating them to their opposites (antonyms).

CCSS.ELA-Literacy.L.K.5d...**The Storytelling Circle** (p. 53)
Distinguish shades of meaning among verbs describing the same general action (e.g., walk, march, strut, prance) by acting out the meanings.

Reading: Foundational Skills

CCSS.ELA-Literacy.RF.K.1d...**Jump Ropes for ELA** (p. 54)
Recognize and name all upper- and lowercase letters of the alphabet.

GRADE 1

Operations & Algebraic Thinking

CCSS.Math.Content.1.OA.D.7............................**"You Get the Equal Sign"** (p. 94)

Understand the meaning of the equal sign, and determine if equations involving addition and subtraction are true or false. For example, which of the following equations are true and which are false? $6 = 6$, $7 = 8 - 1$, $5 + 2 = 2 + 5$, $4 + 1 = 5 + 2$.

Number & Operations in Base Ten

CCSS.Math.Content.1.NBT.B.2...........................**Place Value Hopscotch** (p. 18)

Understand that the two digits of a two-digit number represent amounts of tens and ones.

Place Value Jumping Jacks (p. 22)
And Then Along Came.... (p. 33)

CCSS.Math.Content.1.NBT.B.3...........................**The Hungry Alligator Game** (p. 26)

Compare two two-digit numbers based on meanings of the tens and ones digits, recording the results of comparisons with the symbols >, =, and <.

Geometry

CCSS.Math.Content.1.G.A.2..............................**Jump Ropes for Math** (p. 24)

Compose two-dimensional shapes (rectangles, squares, trapezoids, triangles, half-circles, and quarter-circles) or three-dimensional shapes (cubes, right rectangular prisms, right circular cones, and right circular cylinders) to create a composite shape, and compose new shapes from the composite shape.

GRADE 1

ENGLISH LANGUAGE ARTS

Reading: Informational Text

CCSS.ELA-Literacy.RI.1.5....................................**"The Book Parts Song"** (p. 101)
Know and use various text features (e.g., headings, tables of contents, glossaries, electronic menus, icons) to locate key facts or information in a text.

Reading: Foundational Skills

CCSS.ELA-Literacy.RF.1.4a................................**Reading Comprehension Dribbling** (p. 59)
Read grade-level text with purpose and understanding.

CCSS.ELA-Literacy.RF.1.4b................................**Reading Around the Room** (p. 57)
Read grade-level text orally with accuracy, appropriate rate, and expression on successive readings.

Writing

CCSS.ELA-Literacy.W.1.3....................................**"All of Us Can"** (p. 100)
Write narratives in which they recount two or more appropriately sequenced events, include some details regarding what happened, use temporal words to signal event order, and provide some sense of closure.

Language

CCSS.ELA-Literacy.L.1.1j....................................**Card Sort** (p. 60)
Produce and expand complete simple and compound declarative, interrogative, imperative, and exclamatory sentences in response to prompts.   **Four Types of Sentences** (p. 147)

CCSS.ELA-Literacy.L.1.2a....................................**The Slouch Game** (p. 58)
Capitalize dates and names of people.   **Card Sort** (p. 60)
"Need to Have A Cap" (p. 103)
CSI (p. 145)

CCSS.ELA-Literacy.L.1.5d....................................**The Storytelling Circle** (p. 53)
Distinguish shades of meaning among verbs differing in manner (e.g., look, peek, glance, stare, glare, scowl) and adjectives differing in intensity (e.g., large, gigantic) by defining or choosing them or by acting out the meanings.

GRADE 2

Operations & Algebraic Thinking

CCSS.Math.Content.2.OA.C.3.............................**The Day Steven Got Even** (p. 35)
Determine whether a group of objects (up to 20) has an odd or even
number of members, e.g., by pairing objects or counting them by
2s; write an equation to express an even number as a sum of two
equal addends.

Number & Operations in Base Ten

CCSS.Math.Content.2.NBT.A.1............................**Place Value Hopscotch** (p. 18)
Understand that the three digits of a three-digit number represent   **Place Value Jumping Jacks** (p. 22)
amounts of hundreds, tens, and ones; e.g., 706 equals 7 hundreds, 0   **And Then Along Came...** (p. 33)
tens, and 6 ones.

CCSS.Math.Content.2.NBT.A.3............................**Reading Large Numbers** (p. 27)
Read and write numbers to 1000 using base-ten numerals, number
names, and expanded form.

CCSS.Math.Content.2.NBT.A.4............................**The Hungry Alligator Game** (p. 26)
Compare two three-digit numbers based on meanings of the hun-
dreds, tens, and ones digits, using >, =, and < symbols to record the
results of comparisons.

CCSS.Math.Content.2.NBT.B.5............................**The Subtraction Fire** (p. 30)
Fluently add and subtract within 100 using strategies based on place
value, properties of operations, and/or the relationship between addition and subtraction.

CCSS.Math.Content.2.NBT.B.7............................**The Subtraction Fire** (p. 30)
Add and subtract within 1000, using concrete models or drawings
and strategies based on place value, properties of operations, and/
or the relationship between addition and subtraction; relate the
strategy to a written method. Understand that in adding or subtracting three-digit numbers, one adds or subtracts hundreds and hundreds, tens and tens, ones and ones; and sometimes it is necessary
to compose or decompose tens or hundreds.

Geometry

CCSS.Math.Content.2.G.A.1................................**Jump Ropes for Math** (p. 24)
Recognize and draw shapes having specified attributes, such as a   **"Faces, Edges, Vertices"** (p. 93)
given number of angles or a given number of equal faces. Identify
triangles, quadrilaterals, pentagons, hexagons, and cubes.

GRADE 2

ENGLISH LANGUAGE ARTS

Reading: Literature

CCSS.ELA-Literacy.RL.2.1......................................**The Five Ws Chant** (p. 146)
Ask and answer such questions as who, what, where, when, why, and how to demonstrate understanding of key details in a text.

CCSS.ELA-Literacy.RL.2.4......................................**Alliterations** (p. 143)
Describe how words and phrases (e.g., regular beats, alliteration, rhymes, repeated lines) supply rhythm and meaning in a story, poem, or song.

Reading: Informational Text

CCSS.ELA-Literacy.RI.2.1......................................**The Five Ws Chant** (p. 146)
Ask and answer such questions as who, what, where, when, why, and how to demonstrate understanding of key details in a text.

CCSS.ELA-Literacy.RI.2.5......................................**"The Book Parts Song"** (p. 101)
Know and use various text features (e.g., captions, bold print, sub-headings, glossaries, indexes, electronic menus, icons) to locate key facts or information in a text efficiently.

Reading: Foundational Skills

CCSS.ELA-Literacy.RF.2.3d......................................**Index Card Arranging** (p. 55)
Decode words with common prefixes and suffixes. **"The Prefix-Suffix Song"** (p. 102)

CCSS.ELA-Literacy.RF.2.4a......................................**Reading Comprehension Dribbling** (p. 59)
Read grade-level text with purpose and understanding.

CCSS.ELA-Literacy.RF.2.4b......................................**Reading Around the Room** (p. 57)
Read grade-level text orally with accuracy, appropriate rate, and expression on successive readings.

Writing

CCSS.ELA-Literacy.W.2.3......................................**"All of Us Can"** (p. 100)
Write narratives in which they recount a well-elaborated event or short sequence of events, include details to describe actions, thoughts, and feelings, use temporal words to signal event order, and provide a sense of closure.

Speaking & Listening

CCSS.ELA-Literacy.SL.2.1......................................**The Walking Pair Share** (p. 164)
Participate in collaborative conversations with diverse partners about grade 2 topics and texts with peers and adults in small and larger groups.

Language

CCSS.ELA-Literacy.L.2.2a......................................**The Slouch Game** (p. 58)
Capitalize holidays, product names, and geographic names. **Card Sort** (p. 60)
"Need to Have A Cap" (p. 103)
CSI (p. 145)

GRADE 3

MATH

Operations & Algebraic Thinking

CCSS.Math.Content.3.OA.A.2..................................**Authentic Math** (p. 46)
Interpret whole-number quotients of whole numbers, e.g., interpret 56 **"Now You're A-OK"** (p. 92)
÷ 8 as the number of objects in each share when 56 objects are parti-
tioned equally into 8 shares, or as a number of shares when 56 objects
are partitioned into equal shares of 8 objects each.

CCSS.Math.Content.3.OA.A.3..................................**Authentic Math** (p. 46)
Use multiplication and division within 100 to solve word problems in
situations involving equal groups, arrays, and measurement quantities,
e.g., by using drawings and equations with a symbol for the unknown
number to represent the problem.

CCSS.Math.Content.3.OA.A.4..................................**"You Get the Equal Sign"** (p. 94)
Determine the unknown whole number in a multiplication or division
equation relating three whole numbers.

CCSS.Math.Content.3.OA.C.7..................................**Macarena Math** (p. 98)
Fluently multiply and divide within 100, using strategies such as the relationship between multiplication and division (e.g., knowing that 8 ×
5 = 40, one knows 40 ÷ 5 = 8) or properties of operations. By the end
of Grade 3, know from memory all products of two one-digit numbers.

Number & Operations in Base Ten

CCSS.Math.Content.3.NBT.A.1..................................**Rapid Rounding** (p. 25)
Use place value understanding to round whole numbers to the nearest **Rounding Chant** (p. 149)
10 or 100.

CCSS.Math.Content.3.NBT.A.2..................................**Place Value Hopscotch** (p. 18)
Fluently add and subtract within 1000 using strategies and algorithms **The Subtraction Fire** (p. 30)
based on place value, properties of operations, and/or the relationship
between addition and subtraction.

Number & Operations — Fractions

CCSS.Math.Content.3.NF.A.3d..................................**The Hungry Alligator Game** (p. 26)
Compare two fractions with the same numerator or the same denomi-
nator by reasoning about their size. Recognize that comparisons are
valid only when the two fractions refer to the same whole. Record
the results of comparisons with the symbols >, =, or <, and justify the
conclusions, e.g., by using a visual fraction model.

Measurement & Data

CCSS.Math.Content.3.MD.C.5..................................**The Story of Area** (p. 40)
Recognize area as an attribute of plane figures and understand con- **Area Goes 3-D** (p. 42)
cepts of area measurement.

CCSS.Math.Content.3.MD.D.8..................................**The Story of Peri Meter** (p. 39)
Solve real world and mathematical problems involving perimeters of
polygons, including finding the perimeter given the side lengths, finding
an unknown side length, and exhibiting rectangles with the same perimeter and different areas or with the same area and different perimeters.

Geometry

Understand that shapes in different categories (e.g., rhombuses, rectangles, and others) may share attributes (e.g., having four sides), and that the shared attributes can define a larger category (e.g., quadrilaterals). Recognize rhombuses, rectangles, and squares as examples of quadrilaterals, and draw examples of quadrilaterals that do not belong to any of these subcategories.

GRADE 3

ENGLISH LANGUGE ARTS

Reading: Informational Text

CCSS.ELA-Literacy.RI.3.8...**"Cause and Effect"** (p. 104)
Describe the logical connection between particular sentences and
paragraphs in a text (e.g., comparison, cause/effect, first/second/third
in a sequence).

Reading: Foundational Skills

CCSS.ELA-Literacy.RF.3.3a.......................................**Index Card Arranging** (p. 55)
Identify and know the meaning of the most common prefixes and deriva- **"The Prefix-Suffix Song"** (p. 102)
tional suffixes.

CCSS.ELA-Literacy.RF.3.3b.......................................**Index Card Arranging** (p. 55)
Decode words with common Latin suffixes. **"The Prefix-Suffix Song"** (p. 102)

CCSS.ELA-Literacy.RF.3.4a..............................**Reading Comprehension Dribbling** (p. 59)
Read grade-level text with purpose and understanding.

CCSS.ELA-Literacy.RF.3.4b.......................................**Reading Around the Room** (p. 57)
Read grade-level prose and poetry orally with accuracy, appropriate
rate, and expression on successive readings.

Writing

CCSS.ELA-Literacy.W.3.3...**"All of Us Can"** (p. 100)
Write narratives to develop real or imagined experiences or events using
effective technique, descriptive details, and clear event sequences.

Speaking & Listening

CCSS.ELA-Literacy.SL.3.5...**Reading Around the Room** (p. 57)
Create engaging audio recordings of stories or poems that demonstrate
fluid reading at an understandable pace; add visual displays when appropriate to emphasize or enhance certain facts or details.

Language

CCSS.ELA-Literacy.L.3.1i...**Subject and Predicate** (p. 141)
Produce simple, compound, and complex sentences.

CCSS.ELA-Literacy.L.3.2a...**The Slouch Game** (p. 58)
Capitalize appropriate words in titles. **Card Sort** (p. 60)
"Need to Have A Cap" (p. 103)
CSI (p. 145)

CCSS.ELA-Literacy.L.3.2d...**The Trip to the Zoo** (p. 66)
Form and use possessives.

CCSS.ELA-Literacy.L.3.2e...**Index Card Arranging** (p. 55)
Use conventional spelling for high-frequency and other studied words and **"The Prefix-Suffix Song"** (p. 102)
for adding suffixes to base words (e.g., sitting, smiled, cries, happiness).

CCSS.ELA-Literacy.L.3.2g...**Index Card Arranging** (p. 55)
Consult reference materials, including beginning dictionaries, as
needed to check and correct spellings.

GRADE 4

Number & Operations in Base Ten

CCSS.Math.Content.4.NBT.A.1.................................**Place Value Hopscotch** (p. 18)
Recognize that in a multi-digit whole number, a digit in one place represents ten times what it represents in the place to its right.

CCSS.Math.Content.4.NBT.A.3.................................**Rapid Rounding** (p. 25)
Use place value understanding to round multi-digit whole numbers to **Rounding Chant** (p. 149)
any place.

CCSS.Math.Content.4.NBT.B.4.................................**The Subtraction Fire** (p. 30)
Fluently add and subtract multi-digit whole numbers using the standard algorithm.

CCSS.Math.Content.4.NBT.B.5.................................**The Sprinkler System** (p. 36)
Multiply a whole number of up to four digits by a one-digit whole number, and multiply two two-digit numbers, using strategies based on place value and the properties of operations. Illustrate and explain the calculation by using equations, rectangular arrays, and/or area models.

CCSS.Math.Content.4.NBT.B.6.................................**"Now You're A-OK"** (p. 92)
Find whole-number quotients and remainders with up to four-digit dividends and one-digit divisors, using strategies based on place value, the properties of operations, and/or the relationship between multiplication and division. Illustrate and explain the calculation by using equations, rectangular arrays, and/or area models.

Number & Operations — Fractions

CCSS.Math.Content.4.NF.A.2.................................**The Hungry Alligator Game** (p. 26)
Compare two fractions with different numerators and different denominators, e.g., by creating common denominators or numerators, or by comparing to a benchmark fraction such as 1/2. Recognize that comparisons are valid only when the two fractions refer to the same whole. Record the results of comparisons with symbols >, =, or <, and justify the conclusions, e.g., by using a visual fraction model.

CCSS.Math.Content.4.NF.C.6.................................**Place Value Shuffle** (p. 20)
Use decimal notation for fractions with denominators 10 or 100.

CCSS.Math.Content.4.NF.C.7.................................**The Hungry Alligator Game** (p. 26)
Compare two decimals to hundredths by reasoning about their size. Recognize that comparisons are valid only when the two decimals refer to the same whole. Record the results of comparisons with the symbols >, =, or <, and justify the conclusions, e.g., by using a visual model.

Measurement & Data

CCSS.Math.Content.4.MD.A.1.................................**"The Measurement Conga"** (p. 96)
Know relative sizes of measurement units within one system of units including km, m, cm; kg, g; lb, oz.; l, ml; hr, min, sec. Within a single system of measurement, express measurements in a larger unit in terms of a smaller unit. Record measurement equivalents in a two-column table.

Geometry

CCSS.Math.Content.4.G.A.1.................................**Jump Ropes for Math** (p. 24)
Draw points, lines, line segments, rays, angles (right, acute, obtuse), **"Lines, Rays, and Segments"** (p. 95)
and perpendicular and parallel lines. Identify these in two-dimen- **Three Kinds of Angles** (p. 151)
sional figures.

GRADE 4

ENGLISH LANGUAGE ARTS

Reading: Literature

CCSS.ELA-Literacy.RL.4.1...**Making an Inference** (p. 142)
Refer to details and examples in a text when explaining what the text
says explicitly and when drawing inferences from the text.

Reading: Informational Text

CCSS.ELA-Literacy.RI.4.1...**Making an Inference** (p. 142)
Refer to details and examples in a text when explaining what the text
says explicitly and when drawing inferences from the text.

CCSS.ELA-Literacy.RI.4.5...**"Cause and Effect"** (p. 104)
Describe the overall structure (e.g., chronology, comparison, cause/
effect, problem/solution) of events, ideas, concepts, or information in
a text or part of a text.

Reading: Foundational Skills

CCSS.ELA-Literacy.RF.4.4a...**Reading Comprehension Dribbling** (p. 59)
Read grade-level text with purpose and understanding.

CCSS.ELA-Literacy.RF.4.4b...**Reading Around the Room** (p. 57)
Read grade-level prose and poetry orally with accuracy, appropriate
rate, and expression on successive readings.

Writing

CCSS.ELA-Literacy.W.4.3...**"All of Us Can"** (p. 100)
Write narratives to develop real or imagined experiences or events us-
ing effective technique, descriptive details, and clear event sequences.

Language

CCSS.ELA-Literacy.L.4.1f...**Subject and Predicate** (p. 141)
Produce complete sentences, recognizing and correcting inappropri-
ate fragments and run-ons.

CCSS.ELA-Literacy.L.4.2a...**The Slouch Game** (p. 58)
Use correct capitalization.   **Card Sort** (p. 60)
                                                                 "Need to Have A Cap" (p. 103)
                                                                 CSI (p. 145)

CCSS.ELA-Literacy.L.4.4c...**Index Card Arranging** (p. 55)
Consult reference materials (e.g., dictionaries, glossaries, thesauruses),
both print and digital, to find the pronunciation and determine or
clarify the precise meaning of key words and phrases.

CCSS.ELA-Literacy.L.4.5c...**The Synonym-Antonym Sidestep** (p. 50)
Demonstrate understanding of words by relating them to their oppo-   **The Jumping Game** (p. 52)
sites (antonyms) and to words with similar but not identical meanings
(synonyms).

GRADE 5

Operations & Algebraic Thinking

CCSS.Math.Content.5.OA.B.3...................................**The Farmer's Market** (p. 44)

Generate two numerical patterns using two given rules. Identify apparent relationships between corresponding terms. Form ordered pairs consisting of corresponding terms from the two patterns, and graph the ordered pairs on a coordinate plane.

Numbers & Operations in Base Ten

CCSS.Math.Content.5.NBT.A.1...............................**Place Value Hopscotch** (p. 18)

Recognize that in a multi-digit number, a digit in one place represents **Place Value Jumping Jacks** (p. 22)
10 times as much as it represents in the place to its right and 1/10 of **Place Value Shuffle** (p. 20)
what it represents in the place to its left.

CCSS.Math.Content.5.NBT.A.3...............................**Place Value Shuffle** (p. 20)

Read, write, and compare decimals to thousandths. **The Hungry Alligator Game** (p. 26)

CCSS.Math.Content.5.NBT.A.4...............................**Rapid Rounding** (p. 25)

Use place value understanding to round decimals to any place. **Rounding Chant** (p. 149)

CCSS.Math.Content.5.NBT.B.5...............................**The Sprinkler System** (p. 36)

Fluently multiply multi-digit whole numbers using the standard algorithm.

CCSS.Math.Content.5.NBT.B.7...............................**The Multiplication Hula** (p. 37)

Add, subtract, multiply, and divide decimals to hundredths, using concrete models or drawings and strategies based on place value, properties of operations, and/or the relationship between addition and subtraction; relate the strategy to a written method and explain the reasoning used.

Measurement & Data

CCSS.Math.Content.5.MD.C.3...............................**The Story of Volume** (p. 43)

Recognize volume as an attribute of solid figures and understand concepts of volume measurement.

Geometry

CCSS.Math.Content.5.G.A.1...............................**The Farmer's Market** (p. 44)

Use a pair of perpendicular number lines, called axes, to define a coordinate system, with the intersection of the lines (the origin) arranged to coincide with the 0 on each line and a given point in the plane located by using an ordered pair of numbers, called its coordinates. Understand that the first number indicates how far to travel from the origin in the direction of one axis, and the second number indicates how far to travel in the direction of the second axis, with the convention that the names of the two axes and the coordinates correspond (e.g., x-axis and x-coordinate, y-axis and y-coordinate).

CCSS.Math.Content.5.G.A.2...............................**The Farmer's Market** (p. 44)

Represent real world and mathematical problems by graphing points in the first quadrant of the coordinate plane, and interpret coordinate values of points in the context of the situation.

GRADE 5

ENGLISH LANGUAGE ARTS

Reading: Informational Text

CCSS.ELA-Literacy.RI.5.5...**"Cause and Effect"** (p. 104)
Compare and contrast the overall structure (e.g., chronology, comparison, cause/effect, problem/solution) of events, ideas, concepts, or information in two or more texts.

Reading: Foundational Skills

CCSS.ELA-Literacy.RF.5.4a............................**Reading Comprehension Dribbling** (p. 59)
Read grade-level text with purpose and understanding.

CCSS.ELA-Literacy.RF.5.4b..............................**Reading Around the Room** (p. 57)
Read grade-level prose and poetry orally with accuracy, appropriate rate, and expression on successive readings.

Writing

CCSS.ELA-Literacy.W.5.3...**"All of Us Can"** (p. 100)
Write narratives to develop real or imagined experiences or events using effective technique, descriptive details, and clear event sequences.

Language

CCSS.ELA-Literacy.L.5.4a...**"Cause and Effect"** (p. 104)
Use context (e.g., cause/effect relationships and comparisons in text) as a clue to the meaning of a word or phrase.

CCSS.ELA-Literacy.L.5.4c...**Index Card Arranging** (p. 55)
Consult reference materials (e.g., dictionaries, glossaries, thesauruses), both print and digital, to find the pronunciation and determine or clarify the precise meaning of key words and phrases.

BIBLIOGRAPHY

Asher, James. *Learning Another Language through Actions*. Los Gatos, CA: Sky Oaks Productions, 1996.

Blaydes, Jean. *Thinking On Your Feet: 100+ Activities That Make Learning a Moving Experience*. Murphy, TX: Action Based Learning, 2000.

Burns, Marilyn. *About Teaching Mathematics: A K-8 Resource*. Sausalito, CA: Math Solutions Publications, 2007.

Burns, Marilyn and Susan Ohanian. *Math By All Means: Division Grades 3-4*. Portsmouth, N.H.: Heinemann, 1995.

Dennison, Paul E. and Gail E. Dennison. *Brain Gym® Teacher's Edition*. Ventura, CA: Hearts at Play, Inc., 2010.

Evanski, Gerard A. *Classroom Activators: More Than 100 Ways to Energize Learners*. Thousand Oaks, CA: Corwin Press, 2009.

Gardner, Howard. *Multiple Intelligences: The Theory in Practice*. Alexandria, VA: BasicBooks, 1993.

Gibbs, Jeanne. *Tribes: A Process for Social Development and Cooperative Learning*. Centersource Systems, LLC., 1987.

Guber, Peter. "The Inside Story." *Psychology Today* (March 15, 2011): 79-84.

Hannaford, Carla. *Smart Moves: Why Learning Is Not All in Your Head,* Arlington, VA: Great Ocean Publishers, 1995.

Heiniger-White, Margot C. and Debra Em Wilson. *S'cool Moves for Learning*. Shasta: Integrated Learner Press, 2010.

Hirt, Mary and Irene Ramos. *Maximum Middle School Physical Education*. Champaign, IL: Human Kinetics, 2008.

Lengel, Traci L. and Michael S. Kuczala, eds. *The Kinesthetic Classroom: Teaching and Learning Through Movement,* Thousand Oaks, CA: Corwin Press, 2010.

Mahar, Matthew T., Rhonda A. Kenny, A. Tamlyn Shields, Donna P. Scales, and Gretchen Collins. *Energizers: Classroom-based Physical Activities,* East Carolina University Activity Promotion Laboratory, 2006. www.eatsmartmovemorenc.com/Energizers/Texts/K-5-Energizers.pdf

Schwed, Amy J. and Janice Melichar-Utter. *Brain-Friendly Study Strategies, Grades 2-8: How Teachers Can Help Students Learn,* Thousand Oaks, CA: Corwin Press, 2008.

Tate, Marcia. *Worksheets Don't Grow Dendrites*. Thousand Oaks, CA: Corwin Press, 2010.

Utter, Brenda. *Pick and Plan: 100 Brain-Compatible Lesson Strategies for Lesson Design*. Thousand Oaks, CA: Corwin Press, 2010.

PERMISSIONS

Permission is gratefully acknowledged for use of ideas that were inspirational to the book:

Jean Blaydes www.actionbasedlearning.com
Dave Blackney
Chip Candy
Melanie Champion and the Activity Promotion Laboratory of East Carolina University
www.eatsmartmovemorenc.com/Energizers/Elementary.html Classroom *Energizers* were developed through funding provided by the NC Heath and Wellness Trust Fund to the NC Department of Public Instruction. East Carolina University Activity Promotion Laboratory was contracted to develop the free resource and Be Active NC to disseminate.

Paul Dennison The Cross Crawl and Hook-ups are part of Educational Kinesiology and the Brain Gym® program by Dennison and Dennison, and are used here with permission. Brain Gym® is a registered trademark of Brain Gym® International/The Educational Kinesiology Foundation.

Jerry Evanski drevanski.com
Elly Goldman and Denise Schiavone
Jeff Haebig pinterest.com/wellnessquest/
Mary Hirt
Seth Martin
Rachel O'Donnell
Project Adventure www.pa.org
Marcia Tate
Brenda Utter
Debra Em Wilson www.schoolmoves.com